Versatile Vocabulary

Games for enhancing vocabulary

Jennifer Meldrum
Barbara Reimer

Published by
Garnet Publishing Ltd.
8 Southern Court, South Street,
Reading RG1 4QS, UK

Copyright © 2005 Garnet Publishing Ltd.

This edition first published 2005

The right of Jennifer Meldrum and Barbara Reimer to be identified as the authors of this work has been asserted by them in accordance with the Copyright, Designs and Patents Act 1988.

All rights reserved.
This work is copyright, but copies may be made of the pages with the Photocopiable symbol without fee or prior permission, provided that these copies are used solely within the institution for which the work is purchased. For copying in any other circumstances, prior permission in writing must be obtained from Garnet Publishing Ltd.

British Library Cataloguing-in-Publication Data
A catalogue record for this book is available from the British Library.

ISBN 1 85964 802 9

Production
Project manager:	Richard Peacock
Editorial team:	Helen O'Neill, Lucy Thompson
Art director:	David Rose
Design and typesetting:	Andrea Baker IFA Design Ltd, Plymouth Devon, UK

Special thanks to Bob Reimer for unfailing encouragement and technical advice.

Every effort has been made to trace the copyright holders and we apologize in advance for any unintentional omissions. We will be happy to insert the appropriate acknowledgements in any subsequent edition.

Printed and bound
in Lebanon by International Press

Versatile Vocabulary
Contents

Note from the Authors		4
Notes on Preparation		4
Number Boards and Alphabet Boards		5

Game	Title	Page
1	Alien Attack!	6
2	Race to the Top	12
3	Definition Dice	14
4	Word Patterns	18
5	Word Design Diamonds	28
6	Vocabulary Vortex	36
7	Cue Cubes	42
8	The Secret Word	46
9	What Is the Meaning of this Charade?	50
10	Successful Student	54
11	Lexical Ladder	60
12	Verbal Baseball	68
13	Jigsaw Joinings	74
14	POS Placement	80
15	Parts of Speech Journey	86
16	Close Call	92
17	Creative Categories	96
18	Word Search	100
19	Alphabet Soup	106
20	Five in a Row	110
21	One of a Kind	114
	Word List	117

Note from the Authors

We are happy to share our games with you in *Versatile Vocabulary*. We chose this name because versatility is what excites us most about these games. Some teachers look for vocabulary games because students say they want to widen their vocabulary. For this reason, there are several games for generating vocabulary. There are also games that will expose students to particular sets of words. These games help students feel confident about words they already know and provide a possible list of common words to study.

All of the words we have chosen for the examples and Word List at the end of the book come from various concordances of the most frequently used words. We have identified words we believe ESL/EFL students need to know and have provided simplified, generic definitions. In addition, many of us work in programs that require us to test vocabulary that is already provided from a course book or vocabulary list. Many of our games allow you to practise words that you already use in your classroom.

This book of games requires students to use vocabulary in various ways: defining words, using words in sentences, spelling or acting out words, changing word forms and generating new words.

Notes on Preparation

Some of the games require many cards and thus may take a long time to prepare, but we feel that time spent preparing games that can be used over and over in the classroom is time well spent. We suggest laminating the boards and cards or mounting them on cardboard so that they last. Many games in this book lend themselves well to colour. Colour your boards or copy cards onto coloured paper before laminating or mounting them.

For **place markers** you can use coins, bottle caps, buttons, coloured plastic pieces or coloured paper clips. For **timers** you can use a second hand on a watch or clock, buy a cooking timer or specially made game timer, or use a specified and uniform counting method, such as, "one elephant, two elephants, three elephants …".

Note: Game timers are sometimes hard to find, but we've had success finding them at good game or teaching supply stores, and have even found on-line sites selling timers, along with some interesting dice and place markers.

If you do not have **dice**, you can use number boards instead. When it is a student's turn to roll the die, the student closes his/her eyes and points a finger or a pencil at the board. The number he/she is touching is the number of spaces he/she moves. The other students in the group watch to ensure the student is not choosing the number he/she wants. When a student lands between numbers, the other students in the group judge which number is closest. Give one board to each group instead of a die. Change the boards from time to time. We have included a sheet of number boards for photocopying.

Since a few games also require students to select a letter at random, we have also included three alphabet boards which work in the same way as the number boards. One of them includes only six different letters. The other two contain all 26 letters of the English alphabet.

Number Boards

1	4	5	4	3	6	1	4	2	3
6	3	2	1	4	5	3	2	6	1
2	5	6	3	1	4	2	6	5	6
5	1	3	2	4	6	5	3	2	4
4	6	1	5	3	2	4	5	6	1
3	2	5	1	4	3	6	1	4	5
2	5	3	6	1	4	5	3	2	1
1	4	2	3	5	6	3	1	6	4
6	3	5	4	1	2	4	3	5	2
3	6	4	1	2	5	6	2	1	3

1	3	5	4	1	2	6	5	2	3
2	1	6	3	3	4	2	6	1	5
6	4	2	1	6	3	5	2	6	4
3	5	1	3	2	6	4	1	5	2
5	2	6	4	5	1	3	6	4	5
2	1	4	3	1	5	6	4	1	3
4	6	3	2	5	1	4	5	6	2
2	3	1	5	6	4	2	3	4	5
1	4	2	6	3	5	1	6	2	3
6	5	4	3	2	1	3	2	4	6

5	6	4	1	3	6	5	2	4	1
3	2	5	6	1	4	3	1	6	5
1	3	5	2	4	1	6	1	3	5
4	1	6	3	5	1	2	6	5	4
2	4	1	4	2	3	1	3	1	2
6	5	2	5	6	2	4	5	2	3
5	1	3	4	1	5	3	4	1	6
2	3	6	2	6	3	2	6	2	3
1	4	5	3	4	5	1	5	4	1
5	6	3	4	2	1	6	3	6	2

3	6	5	1	4	2	6	5	3	1
1	4	2	4	6	3	1	4	5	6
5	2	3	6	1	4	5	3	2	3
2	1	6	5	4	3	2	6	5	4
4	3	1	2	6	5	4	2	3	1
6	5	2	1	4	6	3	1	4	2
5	2	6	3	1	4	2	6	5	1
1	4	5	6	2	3	6	1	3	4
3	6	2	4	1	5	4	6	2	5
6	3	4	1	5	2	3	5	1	6

2	6	1	4	3	5	2	1	6	4
6	3	4	5	6	2	1	4	2	3
1	5	2	6	1	3	4	2	1	5
3	4	6	3	2	1	5	6	4	2
4	2	1	5	4	6	3	1	5	4
2	6	5	3	6	4	1	5	6	3
5	1	3	2	4	6	5	4	1	2
2	3	6	4	1	5	2	3	5	4
6	5	2	1	3	4	6	1	2	3
1	4	5	3	2	6	3	2	5	1

1	2	4	6	3	5	1	3	6	4
4	6	5	3	1	6	4	2	5	3
3	1	4	2	5	3	6	3	1	4
5	3	6	1	4	3	2	6	4	5
2	5	3	5	2	1	3	1	3	2
6	4	2	4	6	2	5	4	2	1
4	3	1	5	3	4	1	5	3	6
2	1	6	2	6	1	2	6	2	1
3	5	4	1	5	4	3	4	5	3
4	6	1	5	2	3	6	1	6	2

2	3	6	5	4	1	3	6	2	5
5	4	1	4	3	2	5	4	6	3
6	1	2	3	5	4	6	2	1	2
1	5	3	6	4	2	1	3	6	4
4	2	5	1	3	6	4	1	2	5
3	6	1	5	4	3	2	5	4	1
6	1	3	2	5	4	1	3	6	5
5	4	6	3	1	2	3	5	2	4
2	3	1	4	5	6	4	3	1	6
3	2	4	5	6	1	2	6	5	3

3	1	5	6	2	4	3	5	1	6
1	2	6	4	1	3	5	6	3	2
5	4	3	1	5	2	6	3	5	4
2	6	1	2	3	5	4	1	6	3
6	3	5	4	6	1	2	5	4	6
3	1	4	2	1	6	5	4	1	2
4	5	2	3	6	1	4	6	5	3
3	2	1	6	5	4	3	2	4	6
1	4	3	5	2	6	1	5	3	2
5	6	4	2	3	1	2	3	4	5

4	2	1	6	5	3	4	5	6	1
1	6	3	5	4	6	1	2	3	5
5	4	1	2	3	5	6	5	4	1
3	5	6	4	1	5	2	6	1	3
2	3	5	3	2	4	5	4	5	2
6	1	2	1	6	2	3	1	2	4
1	5	4	3	5	1	4	3	5	6
2	4	6	2	6	4	5	6	2	4
5	3	1	4	3	1	5	1	3	5
1	6	4	3	2	5	6	4	6	2

Alphabet Boards

A–F

D	B	A	F	E	C	D	E	F	A
A	F	C	E	D	F	A	B	C	E
E	D	A	B	C	E	F	E	D	A
C	E	F	D	A	E	B	F	A	C
B	C	E	C	B	D	E	D	E	B
F	A	B	A	F	B	C	A	B	D
A	E	D	C	E	A	D	C	E	F
B	D	F	B	F	D	B	F	B	D
E	C	A	D	C	A	E	A	C	E
A	F	D	C	B	E	F	D	F	B

A–Z

O	S	F	R	D	Z	A	K	M	B
G	E	R	E	L	N	Q	D	U	X
S	P	A	V	I	Y	C	J	T	W
I	F	L	N	B	S	H	N	R	T
H	E	V	R	U	T	4	M	H	P
Y	T	S	K	M	F	E	M	O	G
A	L	R	J	N	C	L	H	I	O
C	W	V	U	E	S	T	G	V	F
H	N	D	Q	O	B	K	D	P	W
S	J	Z	J	X	S	T	C	A	G

A–Z

K	L	R	O	N	T	C	H	V	I
D	A	S	X	J	C	Q	R	Y	P
V	U	W	L	T	G	E	D	S	Z
E	M	J	F	M	U	B	M	L	G
A	U	N	T	I	R	E	K	S	H
Y	F	I	O	D	B	Q	O	L	V
S	F	B	R	G	F	J	W	C	X
Z	N	V	S	T	A	P	J	N	P
R	K	T	H	D	F	U	Z	T	L
Q	Y	I	O	X	S	Y	M	E	W

Photocopiable

Alien Attack!

Game 1

Learning objective: To practise using target words correctly in sentences.

Game objective: To be the first team to circle the sun three times without getting killed by the alien.

Organization: Played as a whole class.

Preparation:
1. Copy one Game Board on an overhead transparency for the class.
2. Copy 1–2 sets of Anti-alien Missile Cards.
3. Copy a Roll Guide Card for each team.
4. Make a list of vocabulary words or a set of vocabulary cards to use in the game. You can "create" more words for a shorter class list by adding different parts of speech of one vocabulary word, or by recycling words in the game.
5. Provide a place marker for each team and a die for the class.

Description of the game:
1. Students are divided into as many as six teams (A–F). The board is placed on an overhead projector. All the place markers start at the labelled Space Stations. Each team stays in one orbit (the orbits are the lines circling the sun).
2. Each team begins with one Anti-alien Missile card.
3. A student from Team A rolls the die. If the roll is a 1, 2, 3 or 4, the teacher moves the marker that number of spaces. The team marker moves from line to line around the sun in the team's orbit – in this case, the 'A' line.
4. If the student rolls a 5, go to step 5 on the Guide. If a student rolls a 6, go to step 6 on the Guide.
5. Without help from his/her team-mates, the student who rolled must use a word chosen by the teacher correctly in a sentence. If he/she is correct, the team's place marker stays where it is. If the student makes a mistake, the team's place marker stays where it is, but the team must return one Anti-alien Missile card to the teacher.
6. If the student rolls a 5, the student does not move and does not answer a question, but the team loses one Anti-alien Missile card.
7. If the student rolls a 6, his/her team are attacked by the alien. If the team has an Anti-alien Missile card, they must give it to the teacher to survive the attack. If the team does not have a card to protect them, they lose their ship and they are out of the game completely.
8. Continue steps 3–7 for teams A-F, moving around the board until one team circles the sun three times. Have players rotate on each team so that every student makes at least one sentence.
9. Each time a team passes their space station, make a note that they have completed one orbit. You can mark this on the board. The first team to orbit three times, or the only team left if the others have been attacked by the alien, wins.
10. A team can trade one orbit point for one Anti-alien Missile card.
11. Give members of teams that have been attacked the option of being picked up by other 'space ships': that is, allow students who are 'out' to join the remaining teams.

Optional: To prevent cheating, if a team-mate tries to help a student or if anyone is caught looking at papers, take away one Anti-alien Missile card. If the team does not have any cards left, take away one orbit point.

Game 1

Variations:
- Have students give definitions instead of using the word in a sentence.
- Make the number rolled a key for the type of word you choose. For example: 1 = noun, 2 = verb, 3 = adjective, 4 = adverb; 1 = module 1 of your course, 2 = module 2 of your course, or 1 = easiest and 4 = most difficult.
- Vary the level of the game by changing the number of orbits the teams need to make or by changing the number of Anti-alien Missile cards the teams begin with.

Note: This game can be played as a large-copy paper version with a small class.

Alien Attack! – Game Board

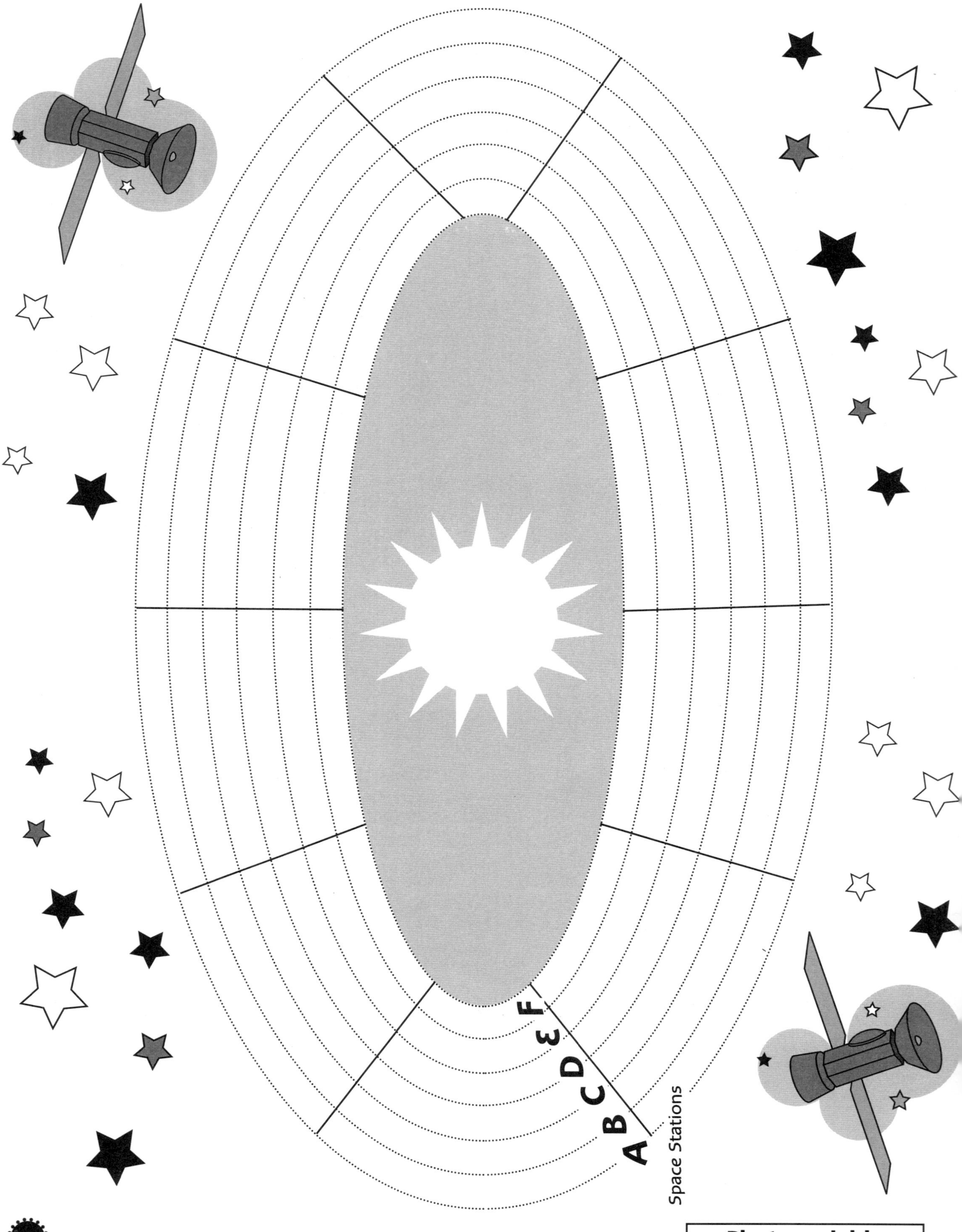

Space Stations

A B C D E F

Photocopiable

Alien Attack! – Students' Roll Guide Cards

If you roll:

1 = move ahead 1 space station and answer

2 = move ahead 2 space stations and answer

3 = move ahead 3 space stations and answer

4 = move ahead 4 space stations and answer

5 = lose 1 Anti-alien Missile card

6 = Alien attacks!

If you roll:

1 = move ahead 1 space station and answer

2 = move ahead 2 space stations and answer

3 = move ahead 3 space stations and answer

4 = move ahead 4 space stations and answer

5 = lose 1 Anti-alien Missile card

6 = Alien attacks!

If you roll:

1 = move ahead 1 space station and answer

2 = move ahead 2 space stations and answer

3 = move ahead 3 space stations and answer

4 = move ahead 4 space stations and answer

5 = lose 1 Anti-alien Missile card

6 = Alien attacks!

If you roll:

1 = move ahead 1 space station and answer

2 = move ahead 2 space stations and answer

3 = move ahead 3 space stations and answer

4 = move ahead 4 space stations and answer

5 = lose 1 Anti-alien Missile card

6 = Alien attacks!

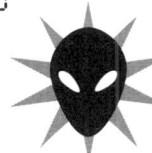

If you roll:

1 = move ahead 1 space station and answer

2 = move ahead 2 space stations and answer

3 = move ahead 3 space stations and answer

4 = move ahead 4 space stations and answer

5 = lose 1 Anti-alien Missile card

6 = Alien attacks!

If you roll:

1 = move ahead 1 space station and answer

2 = move ahead 2 space stations and answer

3 = move ahead 3 space stations and answer

4 = move ahead 4 space stations and answer

5 = lose 1 Anti-alien Missile card

6 = Alien attacks!

Photocopiable

Alien Attack! – Anti-alien Missile Cards

Anti-alien Missile

Anti-alien Missile

Anti-alien Missile

Anti-alien Missile

Anti-alien Missile

Anti-alien Missile

Anti-alien Missile

Anti-alien Missile

Anti-alien Missile

Anti-alien Missile

Anti-alien Missile

Anti-alien Missile

Anti-alien Missile

Photocopiable

Race to the Top!

Learning objective: To practise using target words in sentences.

Game objective: To be the first team to reach the top of the board by using target words correctly.

Organization: Played as a whole class.

Preparation:
1. Copy one board on an overhead transparency for the class.
2. Make a list of vocabulary words or a set of vocabulary cards for the moderator (usually the teacher). You can create more words for a shorter class list by adding alternate parts of speech of one vocabulary word or by recycling words in the game.
3. Provide a place marker for each team.

Description of the game:
1. Students are divided into as many as five teams. The board is placed on an overhead projector. All the place markers start on the bottom of the board.
2. A student from Team A must use a word chosen by the moderator in a sentence, without any help from his/her team-mates. If he/she is correct, the team's place marker is moved to the first space. If not, the place marker stays where it is.
3. The next team (B) has a chance to make a sentence.
4. Repeat steps 2 and 3 for Teams A–E, moving the place markers up the board until one team reaches space 14.
5. If there is a tie, the tied teams continue playing until there is a winner. Alternatively, you can play a 'speed bonus round', where the first team to shout out the correct definition wins.

Optional: To prevent cheating, if a team-mate tries to help a student or if anyone is caught looking at papers, move the offending team's place marker back to the start.

Variations:
- Students must give a definition rather than use the word correctly in a sentence.
- If the first team does not know the answer, allow another team to 'steal' the point.
- Students must spell the target word or give another form of the word (e.g., they are given the verb *teach* and they must give the noun *teacher*).
- Instead of having turns in order, the moderator calls out target words and the first team to give the correct definition moves one step closer to the top. Teams can call out or raise their hands when they believe they have the correct answer.
- If you don't have an OHP, the board can be made large and visible for the class, or simply play the game as a blackboard race without a photocopiable sheet.
- Let students colour in the space when they win a point.

Race to the Top! – Game Board

2.1

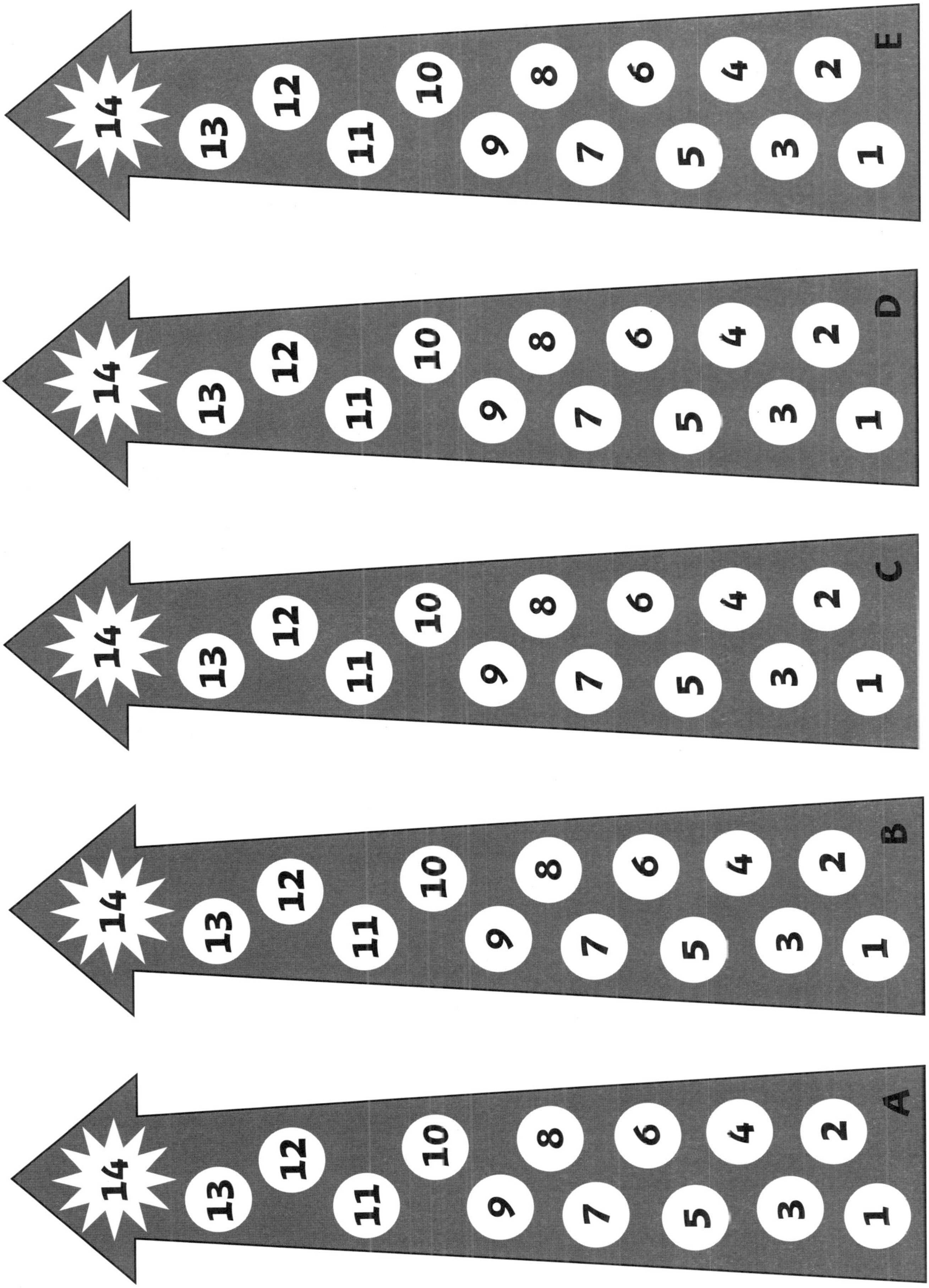

Definition Dice

Game 3

Learning objective: To practise giving definitions of target words.

Game objective: To win the most number of squares.

Organization: Played in pairs or groups of three students.

Preparation:
1. Copy a Game Board for each pair/group of students.
2. Provide a die for each pair/group.

Description of the game:
1. In turn, each student in the group rolls the die. The student finds a box on the board with the number rolled and gives the definition of the word in the box.
2. After the student has defined the word, he/she marks that box with his/her initials or a unique symbol. Each word is defined only once.
3. The other student(s) must judge the accuracy of the definition given. The teacher acts as moderator if there is a dispute. The student with the most boxes wins.

Variations:
- Write the target words for your class in the blank board.
- Instead of defining the word, the students must use it correctly in a sentence or give a different part of speech.

Definition Dice – Game Board

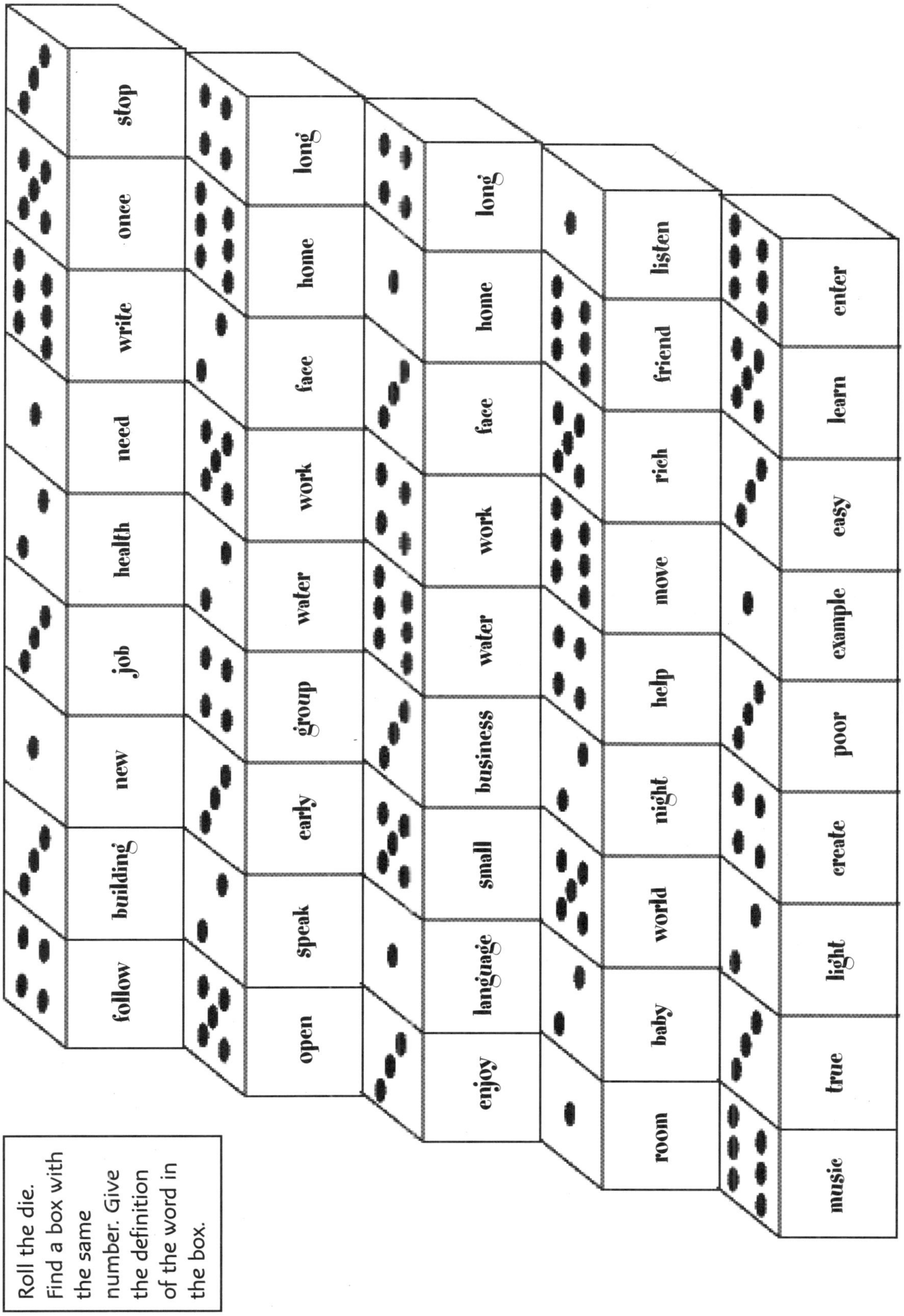

Roll the die. Find a box with the same number. Give the definition of the word in the box.

Die 1	Die 2	Die 3	Die 4	Die 5
stop	long	long	listen	enter
once	home	home	friend	learn
write	face	face	rich	easy
need	work	work	move	example
health	water	water	help	poor
job	group	business	night	create
new	early	small	world	light
building	speak	language	baby	true
follow	open	enjoy	room	music

Photocopiable

Definition Dice – Template

3.2

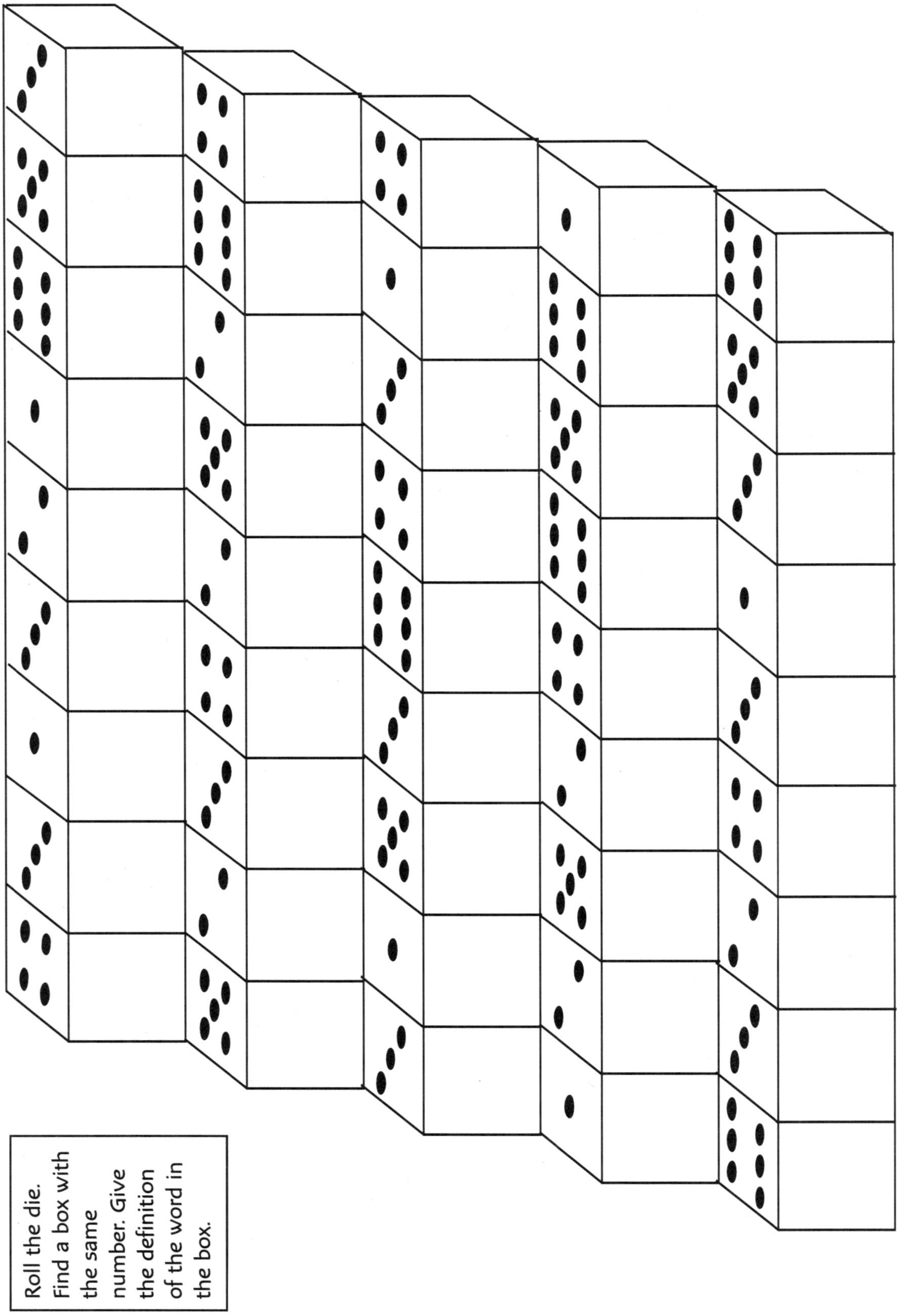

Roll the die. Find a box with the same number. Give the definition of the word in the box.

Photocopiable

Word Patterns

Game  4

Learning objective: To practise giving definitions.

Game objective: To be the first player to reach the end of the board by defining target words correctly.

Organization: Played in small groups of 3–5 students.

Preparation:
1. Copy a Game Board for each small group.
2. Make a set of 20 cards with correct pattern backing for each small group.
3. Provide a die for each group of students and a place marker for each student.

Description of the game:
1. In turn, each student rolls the die and moves his/her place marker the number rolled.
2. He/she takes a vocabulary card with the same patterned back as indicated in the space he/she lands on. The student must give a correct definition of the word on the card.
3. No definition is given on the cards – the other students judge if the definition is correct. This tests the vocabulary knowledge of the other students as well as the student who must provide the definition. The teacher acts as moderator if problems arise.
4. If a student is wrong, he/she must go back two spaces.
5. The first student to reach the End box with an exact roll of the die wins.

Note: Be sure to tell the students what the categories are. Tell them what the different backgrounds of the cards mean. Pattern Key Cards are provided for you to distribute to students to remind them.

Variations:
- Use your own class words. You can divide the cards into any four categories – parts of speech, like the example; into units or chapters from your course, or according to level of difficulty.
  Note: Use the Pattern Key template to show students what the different patterns mean.
- Students have to use the word correctly in a sentence rather than give a definition.
- Have the students spell the words. Another player takes and reads the cards in this case.
- Use the cards from Word Design Diamonds (pages 30 and 32).

Word Patterns – Game Board

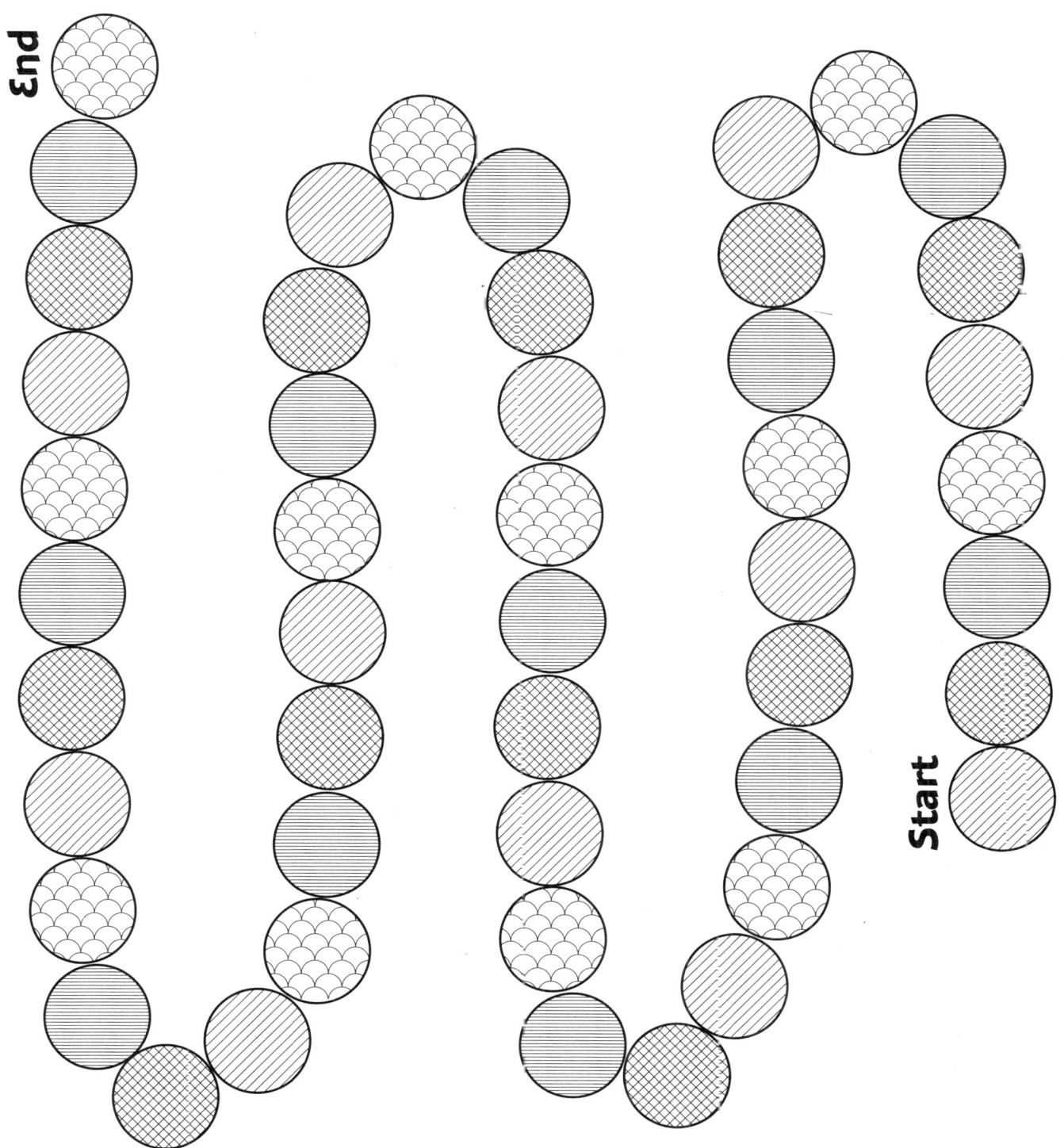

Photocopiable

Word Patterns – Pattern Key Cards

4.2

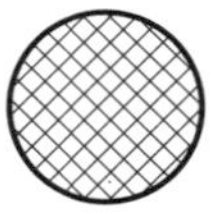

⊕ = Nouns	⊕ = Nouns
⊘ = Verbs	⊘ = Verbs
◉ = Adjectives	◉ = Adjectives
☰ = Adverbs	☰ = Adverbs

⊕ = Nouns	⊕ = Nouns
⊘ = Verbs	⊘ = Verbs
◉ = Adjectives	◉ = Adjectives
☰ = Adverbs	☰ = Adverbs

⊕ = Nouns	⊕ = Nouns
⊘ = Verbs	⊘ = Verbs
◉ = Adjectives	◉ = Adjectives
☰ = Adverbs	☰ = Adverbs

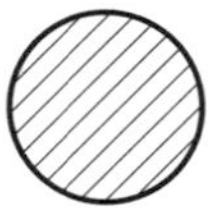

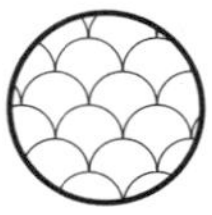

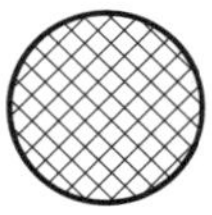

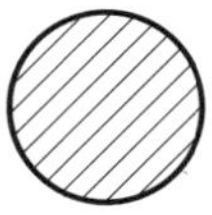

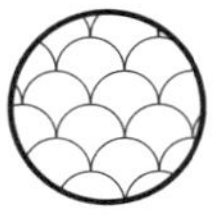

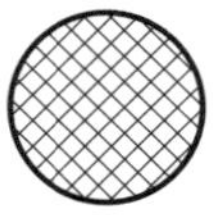

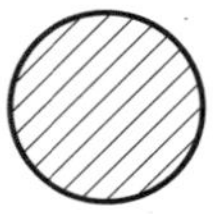

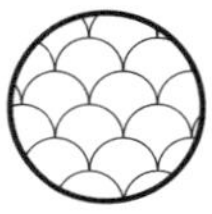

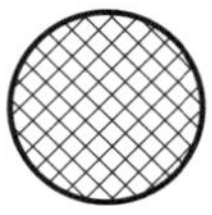

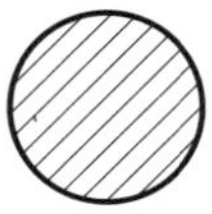

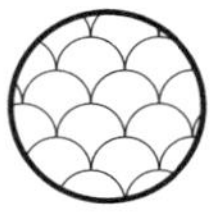

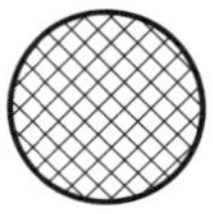

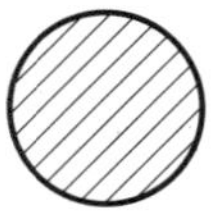

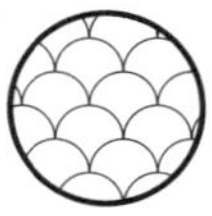

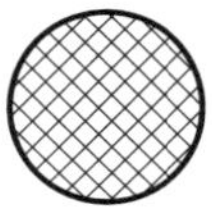

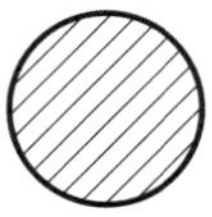

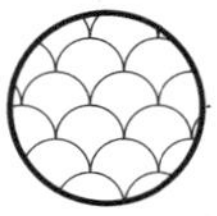

Photocopiable

Word Patterns – Pattern Key Cards

Word Patterns – Cards

4.4

Nouns

association	view	loss	election
objective	relationship	role	involvement
ability	customer	data	solution
memory	realization	revision	demand
behaviour	advantage	design	pressure

Verbs

discuss	forget	happen	notice
raise	review	plan	maintain
develop	explain	generate	recognize
respond	train	remember	define
arise	achieve	consider	evaluate

Photocopiable

Word Patterns – Backing for Cards

Word Patterns – Cards

Adjectives

several	simple	beneficial	central
appropriate	supportive	personal	current
modern	social	successful	difficult
respectful	hopeful	impossible	organized
selective	trustworthy	acceptable	valuable

Adverbs

during	actually	finally	clearly
mainly	obviously	continuously	maybe
decisively	individually	frequently	usually
professionally	necessarily	totally	basically
easily	unbelievably	especially	certainly

Photocopiable

Word Patterns – Backing for Cards

Photocopiable

Word Patterns – Card Template

Word Design Diamonds

Game 5

Learning objective: To practise giving definitions.

Game objective: To be the team to claim the most large diamonds on the game board.

Organization: Played in small groups of 4–6 players.

Preparation:
1. Copy a Game Board for each group.
2. Make a set of cards with correct pattern backing for each group.
3. Provide a different coloured pen or pencil for each group. (For example, one team can use a pencil, the other a blue pen and the third a black pen.)

Description of the game:
1. Each group is divided into two teams of 2–3 students. The two teams share a Game Board. The cards are shuffled and placed beside the board.
2. A student from one team draws a card from the pile of cards. The student must give the definition of the word on the card.
3. If the student gives a correct definition, the team 'claims' a small diamond with a pattern matching the one on the card in an <u>unclaimed</u> larger diamond on the game board. The team colours in the small diamond with the specified team colour and draws another card from the pile. The team must completely claim a large diamond before moving on to another one. For example, if the team draw three nouns in a row but need a verb to complete the larger diamond, they may continue answering to keep control of the game, but they may not claim another small noun diamond until the set of four (noun, verb, adjective and adverb) in one large diamond is completed.
4. The team continue to draw cards until they answer incorrectly or until they have completely claimed a large diamond.
5. Once a large diamond is completely claimed or when a player answers incorrectly, play passes to the other team. All members of the team must rotate in providing answers to provide a chance for all students.
6. The team that claims the most large diamonds wins.

Note: If a team has claimed one of the smaller diamonds of the large diamond, the other team may not claim any small diamonds in the same large diamond (i.e., they cannot 'block' the other team).

Variations:
- Use your own class words. You can use any four categories – parts of speech like the example, units or chapters of your course, or levels of difficulty.
  Note: Tell students what the different patterns on the backs of the cards mean. You can use the Pattern Key Template from Word Patterns.
- Students have to use the word correctly in a sentence rather than give a definition.
- Have the students spell the words. Another player draws and reads the cards in this case.
- Use the cards from Word Patterns on pages 22 and 24.

Word Design Diamonds – Game Board

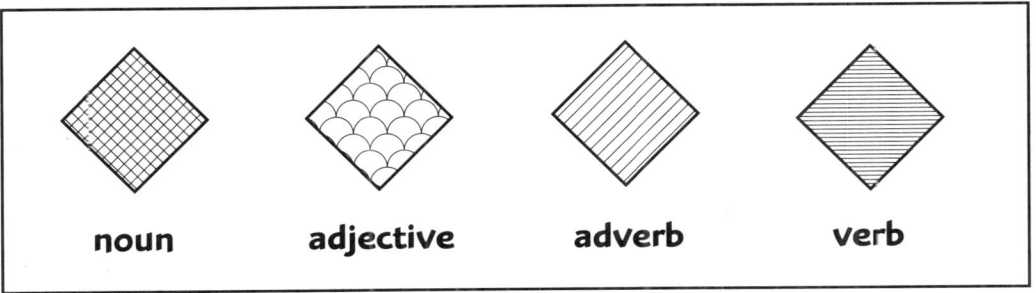

Photocopiable

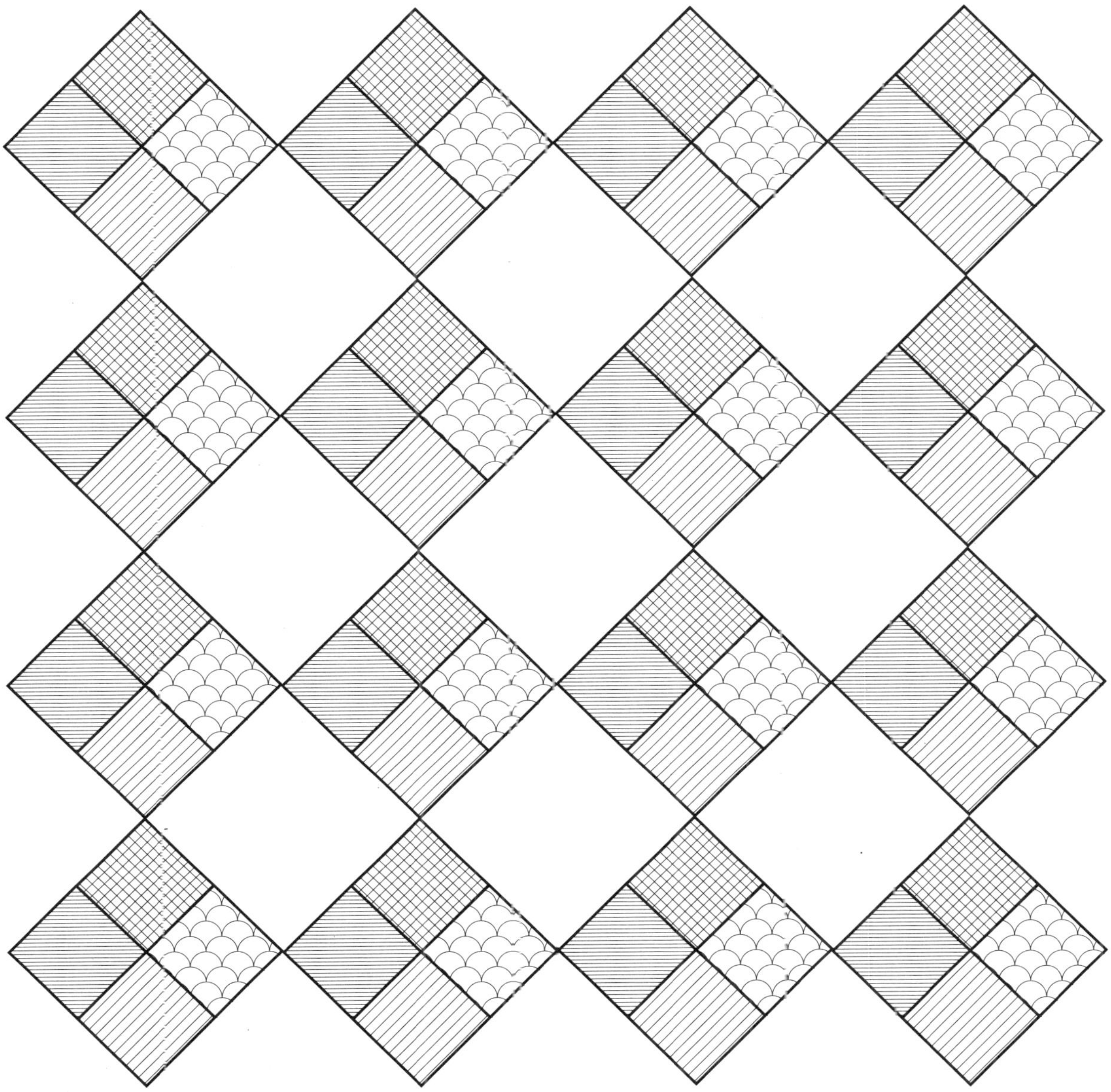

Word Design Diamonds – Cards

5.2

Nouns

utility	compensation	immigration	interaction
layer	aspects	strategies	consequences
variables	assessment	trend	stability
ratio	capacity	code	statistics
phase	simulation	quotation	intervention

Verbs

consult	commit	predict	emerge
confirm	survive	eliminate	convert
guarantee	insert	prohibit	detect
restore	abandon	recover	acknowledge
reinforce	clarify	motivate	exceed

Photocopiable

Word Design Diamonds – Backing for Cards 5.3

Word Design Diamonds – Cards

Adjectives

finite	comprehensive	contrary	unique
classical	ambiguous	neutral	cooperative
flexible	crucial	enhanced	underlying
dominant	technical	valid	perceived
financial	liberal	modified	objective

Adverbs

virtually	eventually	inevitably	minimally
primarily	capably	expertly	definitely
ultimately	identically	thereby	arbitrarily
chiefly	uniformly	tensely	dramatically
predominantly	randomly	radically	visibly

Photocopiable

Word Design Diamonds – Backing for Cards 5.5

Photocopiable

Word Design Diamonds – Card Template

5.6

Vocabulary Vortex

Game

Learning objective: To practise giving definitions.

Game objective: To collect the most vocabulary cards by correctly defining words.

Organization: Played in small groups of 3–6 students.

Preparation:
1. Copy a Game Board for each group.
2. Provide a die for each group and a place marker for each student.
3. Make three different sets of cards for each group – in the example they are nouns, adjectives and verbs. See *Optional* preparation (below).

Optional: This game works nicely in colour. Diamonds are blue, stars are yellow, hearts are red and triangles are green. Print the vocabulary cards on coloured paper to match the category colours and get students to colour the shapes on the board.

Description of the game:
1. The cards are placed face down in the corresponding hexagons. (See Step 3.)
2. To begin, each student places his/her place marker on the space with a triangle closest to him/her.
3. In turn, each student rolls the die and moves his/her place marker the number rolled in *any* direction. The student chooses the shape he/she wants to land on by category. The shape/shapes indicate different categories. For the example game, diamonds represent nouns, stars represent verbs and hearts represent adjectives. If a student lands on a triangle, he/she can choose a card from any of the other three categories.
4. When a student lands on a shape, he/she takes a vocabulary card from the matching category. The student must give a correct definition of the word on the card. No definition is given on the cards. The other students judge if the definition is correct. This tests the vocabulary knowledge of the other students as well as the student who must provide the definition. The teacher acts as moderator if problems arise.
5. If a student is correct, he/she keeps the card.
6. If a student is wrong, he/she places the card in the 'used cards' hexagon.
7. If a student lands on a shape but there are no more cards in that category, he/she cannot try a different card. He/she loses his/her turn. Play until all the cards are either won by students or placed in the used-cards hexagon. The student with the most cards wins.

Note: Tell the students what the categories are and what the different backgrounds mean.

Variations:
- This game works really well with your own target words. You can divide the cards into any three categories – parts of speech (as in the example), units or chapters of your course or levels of difficulty.
- Allow students to 'steal' the card. If the student playing guesses incorrectly, the student who corrects him/her gets to keep the card. If the student playing admits to not knowing the word, the first student to call out the correct definition can keep the card.
- Students have to use the word correctly in a sentence rather than give a definition.
- Have a student spell the word. Another player draws and reads the cards in this case.
- Instead of students playing as individuals, each place marker can represent a pair of students.

Vocabulary Vortex – Game Board

6.1

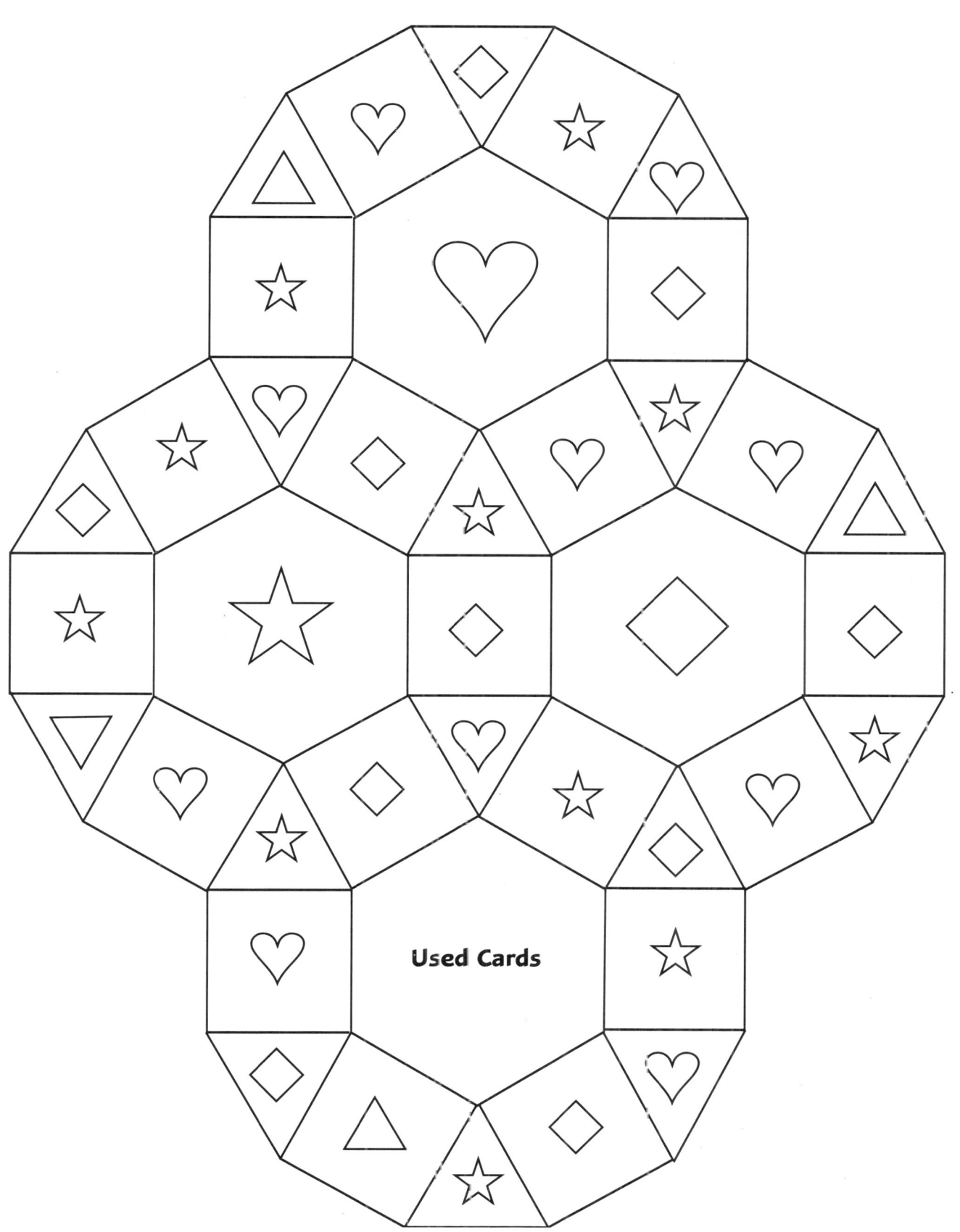

Photocopiable

Vocabulary Vortex – Cards

6.2

Diamond Cards (blue) Nouns

habit
map
knowledge
guard
power
absence
witness
insect
thunder
insult
cliff
basket
bribe
ambition
century
bundle
desert
collar
feather
flavour
medicine
leaf
mercy
lodging
journey
liquid
prejudice
mystery
sympathy
razor
baggage
conversation

Photocopiable

Vocabulary Vortex – Cards

Game
6.3

Star Cards (yellow) Verbs

- perform
- produce
- scold
- quarrel
- tempt
- guess
- relieve
- boast
- mend
- worry
- inquire
- calculate
- annoy
- admire
- invite
- behave
- confess
- float
- explode
- earn
- imagine
- forgive
- manage
- knock
- retire
- multiply
- repeat
- urge
- warn
- descend
- beat
- wrap

Photocopiable

Vocabulary Vortex – Cards

6.4

Heart Cards (red) Adjectives

- exact
- extra-ordinary
- favourite
- awkward
- tame
- jealous
- faint
- sudden
- responsible
- physical
- steady
- straight
- coarse
- evil
- flat
- empty
- tender
- idle
- firm
- instant
- loyal
- humble
- guilty
- miserable
- splendid
- proud
- permanent
- sore
- precious
- ugly
- tight
- pale

Photocopiable

Vocabulary Vortex – Template

Photocopiable

Cue Cubes

Game

Learning objective: To practise using or manipulating target words in six different ways.

Game objective: To earn points by following commands.

Organization: Played as a class or in small groups.

Preparation: Make a cue cube (cut out the cube on the opposite page and paste it together). If your class is playing in small groups, make a cube for each small group.

Description of the game:
1. Divide the class into two teams, A and B. A student from Team A rolls the cube and reads the command that is on top when it lands.
2. A student from Team B selects a word for which the student from Team A must perform the command. For example, if the Team A student rolls *Spell*, the student from Team B can choose a difficult word to spell. The word can be from a class word list or a word the student knows. However, the student giving the word must know the correct answer – he/she cannot just choose a word from a dictionary. He/she must be able to say if the answer is correct or not and must be able to provide the correct answer if asked. The teacher acts as moderator.
3. If the student from Team A performs the command correctly, the team gets one point. Then a student from Team B must roll for a command and a student from Team A selects a word.
4. Students can challenge the knowledge of members of the other team if they think a student does not know the answer for the word he/she has chosen.
5. Keep playing until every student has either a) given a command, b) followed a command, or c) until a team wins a predetermined number of points.

Note: 'Give another form of the word' means that the student must give a different part of speech (e.g., *persuade* can become *persuasive* or *persuasion*).

Variations:
- Students play in small groups.
- Make your own cube from the blank template with different commands.
- You can make a 'word cube' from the blank template, thereby limiting the choice of words to six.

Cue Cubes – Command Cube

7.1

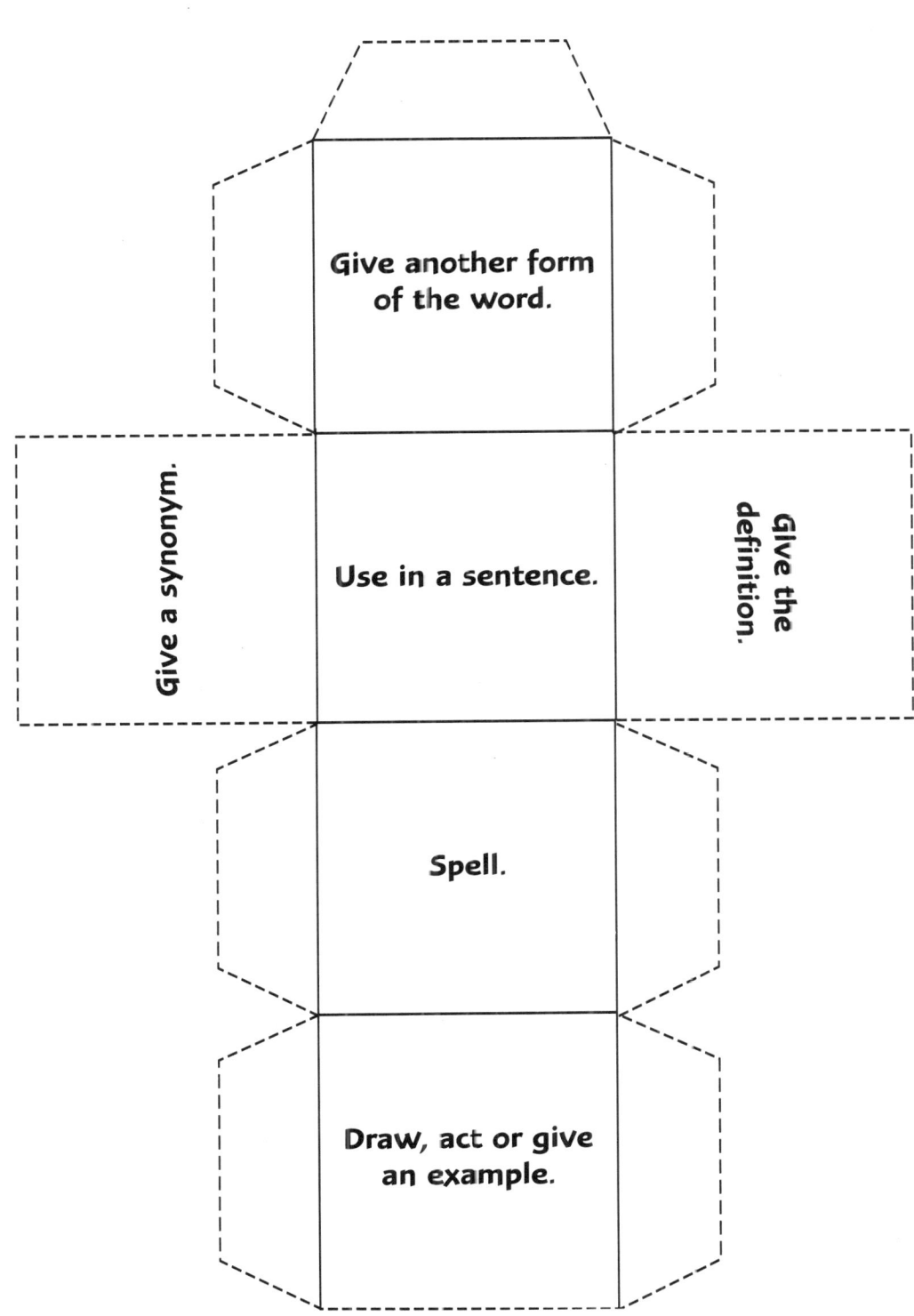

Photocopiable

Cue Cubes – Template

7.2

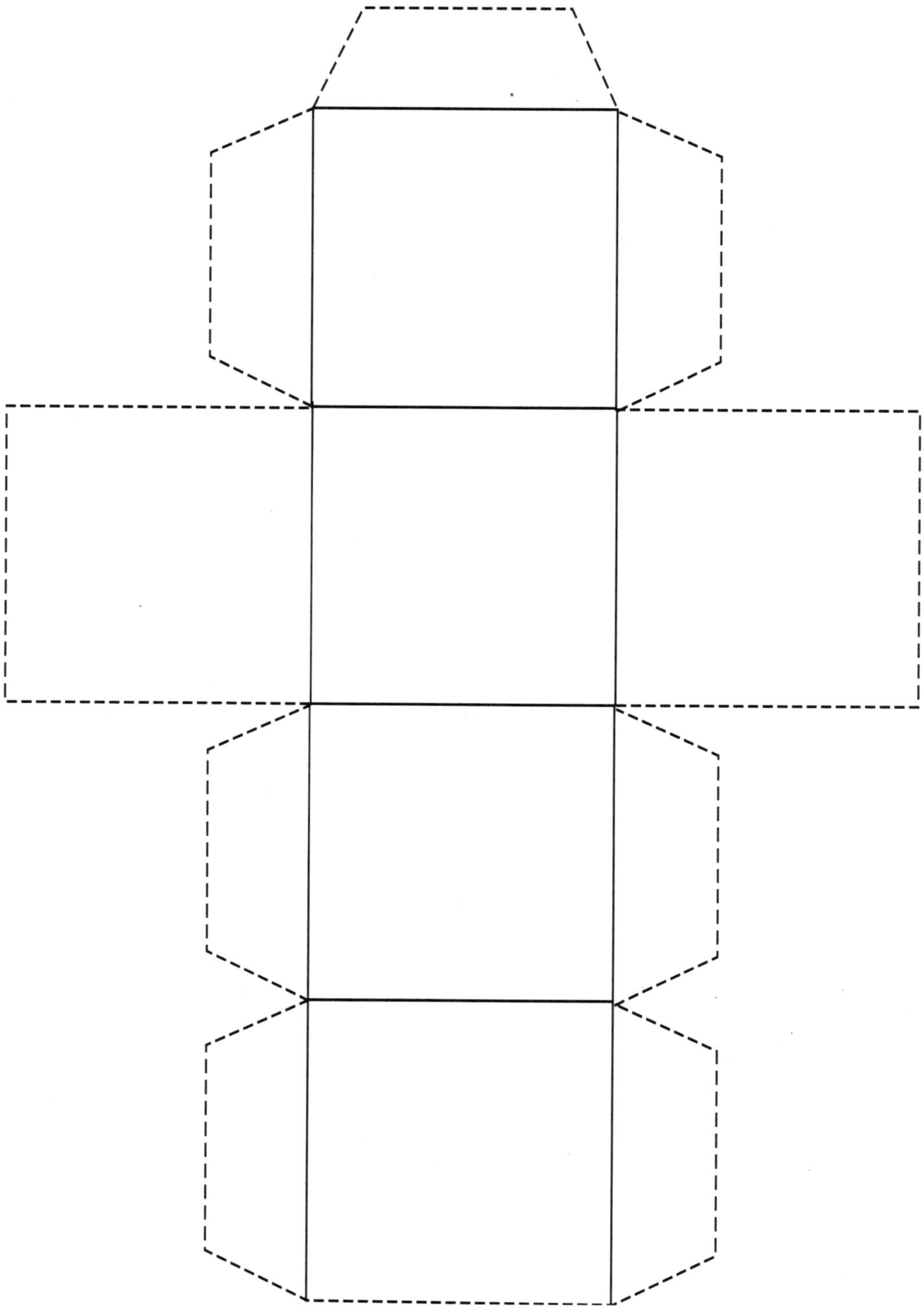

Photocopiable

The Secret Word

Game

Learning objective: To practise defining a word by giving a meaning or example.

Game objective: To win the most points by guessing the most target words successfully.

Organization: Played as a whole class.

Preparation:
1. Copy the Game Board on an overhead transparency for the class.
2. Provide a watch or clock with a second hand or a timer.
3. Copy a number board and an A–F alphabet board from the front of this book.

Description of the game:
1. The class is divided into two or three teams. The board is placed on an overhead projector.
2. A student from the first team comes to the front of the class. The student chooses a 'code' by selecting a number and letter randomly from the number and alphabet boards. The teacher looks at the number and letter selected, but neither the teacher nor the student reveals the information to the other students. The teacher writes down the code (e.g., *B3*) on a piece of paper that is kept out of sight of the rest of the class. This is to prevent the student cheating by trying to change the word.
3. The student looks at the Game Board to find the word that corresponds to the letter and number he/she chose (e.g., *B3* is *destination*).
4. The student at the front of the room has 30 seconds to define the word for his/her team.
   Note: Have the other team keep track of the time. They can signal when the student who is defining the word should start and finish.
5. The team have only one chance to guess the word that is being defined. They should talk about it and choose one word. If a student blurts out a guess, that word is taken as the team's answer.
6. If the guess is correct, the team wins one point. If it is wrong, they <u>lose</u> a point. If the team does not guess in 30 seconds, the team neither gains nor loses a point.
7. Steps 2–6 are repeated for the other team(s).
8. The game is played until every student has come to the front of the class at least once. It is possible to repeat words.

Variations:
- Use the blank board to make your own version. Use words that are similar to each other to make the game more challenging.
  Note: It's easier if you use the same part of speech.
- Change the time students have to guess the answer. Alternatively, change the rules for who can answer from a team: take turns in seating order or select a representative.
- Allow students to mime only, without speaking – good for verbs or adverbs.
- For more teacher control and less chance of word repetition, the teacher can secretly tell the student which word to define rather than using the number and alphabet boards.

The Secret Word – Game Board

	1	2	3	4	5	6
A	climate	chance	evidence	occupation	location	nature
B	border	area	destination	majority	economy	ceremony
C	event	agreement	celebration	environment	arrangement	tradition
D	origin	population	trade	opportunity	promise	reaction
E	surface	resident	maximum	connection	career	combination
F	cause	culture	division	effect	comparison	similarity

Photocopiable

The Secret Word – Template 8.2

	1	2	3	4	5	6
A						
B						
C						
D						
E						
F						

Photocopiable

What Is the Meaning of this Charade?

Game

Learning objective: To generate words and to practise paraphrasing and guessing words from definitions or examples.

Game objective: To be the first team to reach the end of the board by defining and guessing words.

Organization: Played in groups of 4–9 students.

Preparation:
1. Provide blank paper for students to make vocabulary cards. The cards should be 3cm x 3cm. You can cut the paper into cards beforehand or have students cut the cards out themselves. (See Step 1 in Description of the game.)
2. Copy a Game Board for each group. Groups are made up of two or three teams with 2–3 students in each team.
3. Provide a die for each group of students and a place marker for each team of 2–3 students.
4. Ensure each group has a watch or clock with a second hand or a timer (or an alternative fair way of counting time).

Description of the game:
1. Divide the class into teams of 2–3 students. As a team, students make vocabulary cards. Each team writes 10 adjectives, 10 verbs and 10 nouns on the cards. They should intentionally make them difficult to define. Keep the cards with each part of speech separate. For organization, it is easier to have the teams make each part of speech a different colour, either by using different coloured pens or different coloured paper.
   Note: Since Step 1 can be time-consuming, you can have students prepare cards in a class prior to the day you intend to play the game. This gives you the opportunity to check the cards before students play.
2. Put the teams together to form larger groups of two or three teams. Give each group a copy of the Game Board and die. Give each team a place marker.
3. If the cards are made by the class, the teacher collects and redistributes them amongst the groups. Each <u>group</u> gets at least two sets of cards – from two or more <u>teams</u>.
4. Students place the new cards face down in the appropriate spaces on the board (e.g., adjectives go in the space labelled *Adjective Cards*). Each team puts its place marker on START. Students determine which team starts. One student from Team A rolls the die and moves the number indicated.
5. If the student lands on a verb space, he/she picks up a verb card and, without showing the other members of the team, gives a definition or example of the word on the card. The other members of the team have 30 seconds to guess the correct word. The other team(s) keep track of the time and tell the student who is defining the word when to start and finish.
6. If the word is guessed correctly, another student from the team may roll the die and move the number indicated but he/she does not take another card until the *next turn*. If no one guesses the word correctly, the team must stay on that space and in the next turn try to guess another card in the same category. Other teams may not guess the word.
7. Whether a team has guessed correctly or not, the turn passes to the next team on the left. The student who paraphrases or gives examples must change each time a team is playing.

Game 9

Variations:
- Use target words from your course. Do not have students prepare the cards in Step 1 – make the cards in advance instead.
- For weaker classes, either make the vocabulary cards or check the students' cards to ensure the parts of speech are accurate.
- Change the time limit each team has to guess a word.
- Add a "no miming" rule. If a student physically acts out a word instead of/in addition to speaking, the team's place marker is sent back to the start.
- Change the meaning of the symbols. For example, household items or places, sports or health-related words, famous names in art and literature, or famous movies and books.

What Is the Meaning of this Charade? – Game Board

9.1

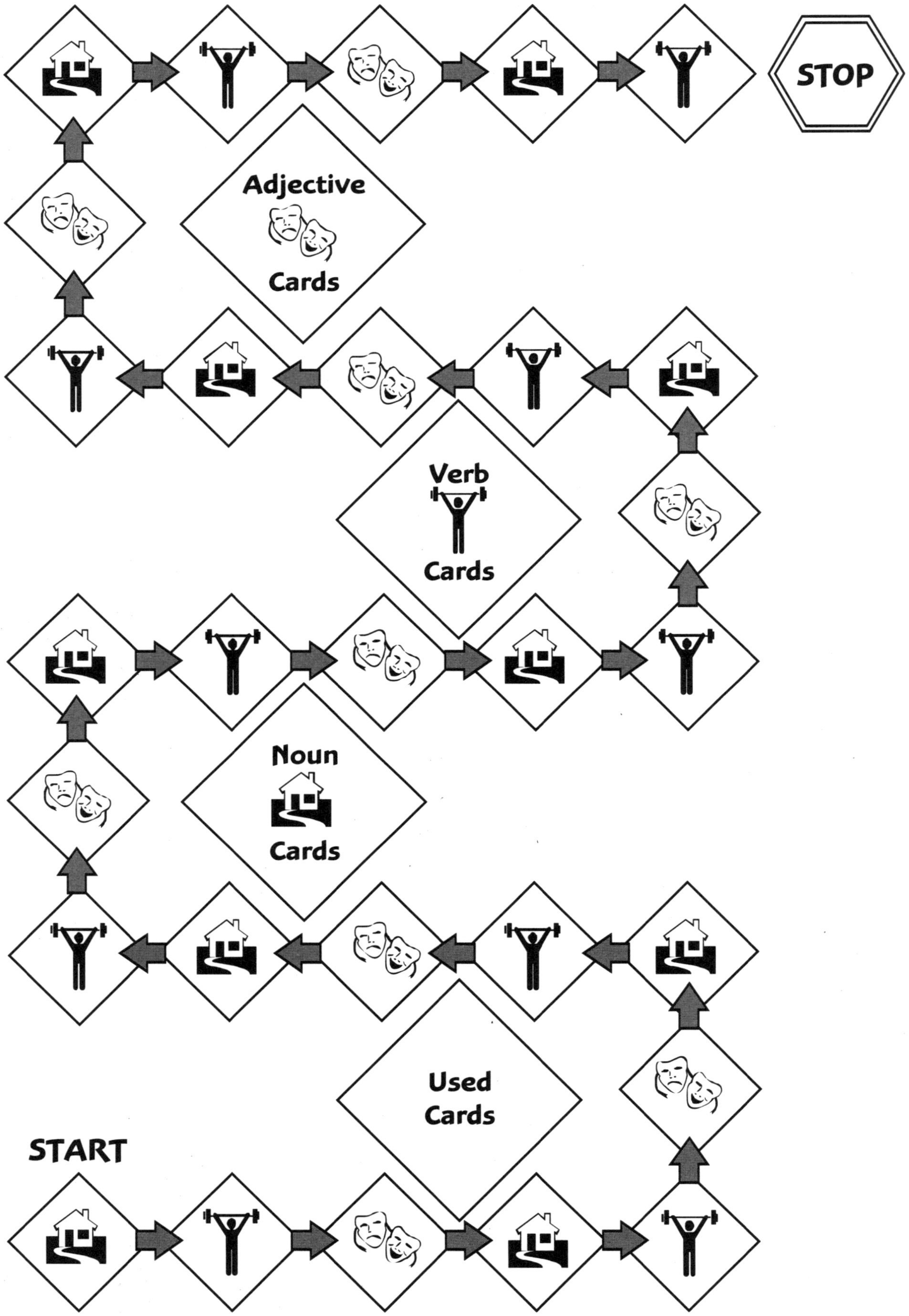

Successful Student

Game 10

Learning objective: To practise giving definitions, spelling words and answering questions about prefixes and suffixes.

Game objective: To be the first player to collect five definition points, five prefix/suffix points and five spelling points.

Organization: Played in small groups.

Preparation:
1. Copy a Game Board. If possible, enlarge the board onto A3 paper and laminate it so you can use it over and over again.
2. Copy one set of definition, prefix/suffix and spelling cards for each group of 3–5 students.
   Note: It is easier for students if the various cards are distinguished from each other by copying them on different coloured paper or card (for example, definition cards on green, prefix/suffix cards on blue).
3. Copy a score card for each student.
4. Provide a die for each group and a place marker for each student.

Description of the game:
1. Each group places cards face down in the appropriate spaces on the board (definition cards in the space marked "definition cards", etc.). Students start by placing their markers on START.
2. One student rolls the die and moves his/her marker to the left. The student does as he/she is instructed on the board. If a player is told to try a card, the student on the player's right picks up the card and reads the question. The same student (on the right) determines if the player's answer is correct or not.
3. If the player answers correctly, he/she writes a point on his/her scorecard. If the player answers incorrectly, he/she neither wins nor loses a point. The turn passes to the student on the left.
4. After a question card has been answered, right or wrong, it is returned to the bottom of the pile. If a student lands on a picture corner space, he/she does nothing.
5. If a student lands on an arrow space, he/she may answer a card (as specified in the space). If he/she answers correctly, he/she wins a point in that category and may enter the smaller trail. If a student lands on a space that causes him/her to lose a point, he/she must erase the point from his/her scorecard.
6. The first student to collect 15 points in total (five definition points, five prefix/suffix points and five spelling points) is the winner.
   Note: The winner must have five of each category, not just 15 points total.

Variations:
- Make your own question cards to reflect the vocabulary you have taught in your own class.
- You do not need to provide the definitions on the cards. Let students judge for themselves if the definition is correct.
- For the prefix/suffix cards, you can write a word with a prefix or suffix underlined. Players must
   a) tell the others what the suffix/prefix is and/or means *or*
   b) identify the part of speech of the word by the suffix *or*
   c) provide the antonym by changing the prefix.
- To change the length of time this game will take, change the number of points required to win (e.g., each student must receive 9 points total – three in each category). Alternatively, do not insist on students getting a particular number of points in each category – allow any 15-point total to win.

Successful Student – Game Board

Successful Student – Definition Cards

CLIENT: (n) customer; a person who pays for your services	PREFERENCE: (n) something you like better than another thing	SUFFER: (v) to have a bad experience; to be in pain
REMAIN: (v) to stay behind	CONDITION: (n) the state something is in; how something looks or feels	MENTAL: (adj) related to the mind
OPINION: (n) your belief or ideas	QUALIFY: (v) to have the ability needed to do something	RECOMMEND: (v) to tell others one thing is better than another; to tell others something is good
IDEAL: (adj) perfect	CONTROL: (n) the power or ability to make people do what you want (v) to have power over someone or something	RESPOND: (v) to answer or react to something
RECENT: (adj) not long ago	ECONOMIC: (adj) related to money, business or industry	AVAILABLE: (adj) not busy; free to use
AVOID: (v) to keep away from	CATEGORY: (n) a group of similar things	SECURE: (adj) safe
ACTIVE: (adj) busy or energetic	RESIST: (v) try not to do; act against	ILLEGAL: (adj) against the law; not permitted by the government
PER CENT: (n) number in each 100	SECTION: (n) a part of a group, place or thing	PARTICULAR: (adj) exact or specific; known
POSSIBLE: (adj) can be done	APPROACH: (v) to come nearer to someone or something	COMMUNITY: (n) people who belong to the same group or live in the same place
GLIMPSE: (n) a short, quick view (v) to take a quick look	ACCURATE: (adj) exactly right	PERIOD: (n) amount of time

Photocopiable

Successful Student – Prefix/Suffix Cards

Change the suffix in the word **useful** to make it mean the opposite. Answer: use<u>less</u>	Add a prefix to **appear** to mean the opposite. Answer: <u>dis</u>appear	What is the prefix or suffix in the word **semicircle** that means **half**? Answer: semi
Change the prefix in **import** to mean the opposite. Answer: <u>ex</u>port	Find the noun: **persuade, persuasively, persuasion, persuasive**. Answer: persuasion	Add a suffix to **health** to make it an adjective. Answer: health<u>y</u>
Add a prefix to **read** to make it mean **read again**. Answer: <u>re</u>read	Add a suffix to **constant** to make it an adverb. Answer: constant<u>ly</u>	Change the prefix in the word **predate** to make it mean the opposite. Answer: <u>post</u>date
Find the verb: **decision, decide, decisive, decidedly**. Answer: decide	What is the prefix or suffix in the word **bicycle** that means **two**? Answer: bi	What is the prefix or suffix in the word **inventor** that means **person who does**? Answer: or
Find the adjective: **active, activity, action, actively**. Answer: active	What is the adjective form of the word **danger**? Answer: danger<u>ous</u>	What is the prefix or suffix in the word **telescope** that means **at a distance**? Answer: tele
Add a prefix to **regular** to mean, **not regular**. Answer: <u>ir</u>regular	What is the noun form of the word **important**? Answer: impor<u>tance</u>	Change the suffix in **careless** to mean the opposite. Answer: care<u>ful</u>
Add a prefix to **correct** to mean **not correct**. Answer: <u>in</u>correct	What suffix makes an adjective into an adverb? Answer: ly	Change the prefix in **export** to mean the opposite. Answer: <u>im</u>port
Add a prefix to **agree** to mean **not agree**. Answer: <u>dis</u>agree	Add a suffix to **reject** to make it into a noun. Answer: rejec<u>tion</u>	Find the adverb: **quickest, quick, quickly, quicker**. Answer: quick<u>ly</u>
What prefix or suffix in the word **subzero** means **below**? Answer: sub	What prefix or suffix in **transport** means **across**? Answer: trans	Add a suffix to the word **neighbour** to make it a thing instead of a person. Answer: neighbour<u>hood</u>
Add a suffix to **broke** to make it an adjective. Answer: brok<u>en</u>	What two parts of speech use the suffix **ive**? Answer: nouns and adjectives	Add a suffix to the word **art** to make it a person instead of a thing. Answer: art<u>ist</u>

Photocopiable

Successful Student – Spelling Cards

Spell the following word: SINCERELY	Spell the following word: DISCUSSION	Spell the following word: OCCASIONALLY
Spell the following word: JUDGMENT	Spell the following word: DOUBT	Spell the following word: DANGEROUS
Spell the following word: BEAUTIFUL	Spell the following word: DISEASE	Spell the following word: SUGGESTION
Spell the following word: KNOWLEDGE	Spell the following word: ENVIRONMENT	Spell the following word: FOREIGN
Spell the following word: SUCCEED	Spell the following word: ACCIDENTALLY	Spell the following word: INTELLIGENCE
Spell the following word: ACCEPTABLE	Spell the following word: ROUGH	Spell the following word: NECESSARY
Spell the following word: PROCEDURE	Spell the following word: EXCITEMENT	Spell the following word: BICYCLE
Spell the following word: ACCURATE	Spell the following word: DISAPPEAR	Spell the following word: SYMBOL
Spell the following word: STRATEGY	Spell the following word: SIMILAR	Spell the following word: ACHIEVEMENT
Spell the following word: SITUATION	Spell the following word: ADAPTABLE	Spell the following word: QUALIFICATION

Photocopiable

Successful Student – Score Cards

Name: _____

Definition points:

Prefix/suffix points:

Spelling points:

Name: _____

Definition points:

Prefix/suffix points:

Spelling points:

Name: _____

Definition points:

Prefix/suffix points:

Spelling points:

Name: _____

Definition points:

Prefix/suffix points:

Spelling points:

Photocopiable

Lexical Ladder

Game 11

Learning objective: To practise using or manipulating target words in four different ways.

Game objective: To be the first to reach the Winner's Circle, moving through four levels of difficulty by correctly answering questions about target words.

Organization: Played in small groups.

Preparation:
1. Copy a Game Board and set of question cards for each group of 4–6 students.
2. Provide a die for each small group and a place marker for each student.

Description of the game:
1. The aim is to move to the Winner's Circle by correctly answering questions at the four levels below. Students can move left or right in each level, but never down a level. The students can only move up a level by correctly answering a question when they land on a box with a star in it.
2. All students begin with their place markers on the Enter Here space. One student rolls the die and moves either left or right around the circle of the first level. The letter on the space determines what kind of question the student must answer: S = spelling, D = definition, WF = word form, P/S = prefixes/suffixes.
3. *Another* student takes a card from the appropriate pile of cards and reads the Level 1 question.
4. If the first student answers correctly, he/she can continue playing. If the student was in a box with a star in it, he/she may move up to Level 2. If the student was not in a box with a star, he/she must continue moving left or right in Level 1 (trying to land on the star box). The student keeps playing until he/she gets a question wrong. Then the turn moves to the next student.
5. If a student moves up to Level 2, then the other student should read a Level 2 question (and at Level 3, a Level 3 question, and so on).
6. Students try to work up to the Winner's Circle. When a student lands in the Winner's Circle, he/she must answer a Level 4 question of the type that the other students agree on (spelling, definition, word form or prefixes/suffixes). The student wins if he/she correctly answers the question.
7. If the student answers incorrectly, he/she must answer a new Level 4 question in the next round.

Variations:
- Two different Game Boards are provided. For a shorter game, copy Game Board 1, with two stars on each level. For a longer game, copy Game Board 2, with one star on each level. For an even shorter game, allow students to move up a level if they get any question correct.
- Play as a class with an OHT and teams.
- Allow students to work in teams of two instead of as individual students.
- Use the cards from Verbal Baseball on page 71.

Lexical Ladder – Game Board 1

Enter Here

S = Spelling
D = Definition
WF = Word Form
PS = Prefix/Suffix

Winner's Circle

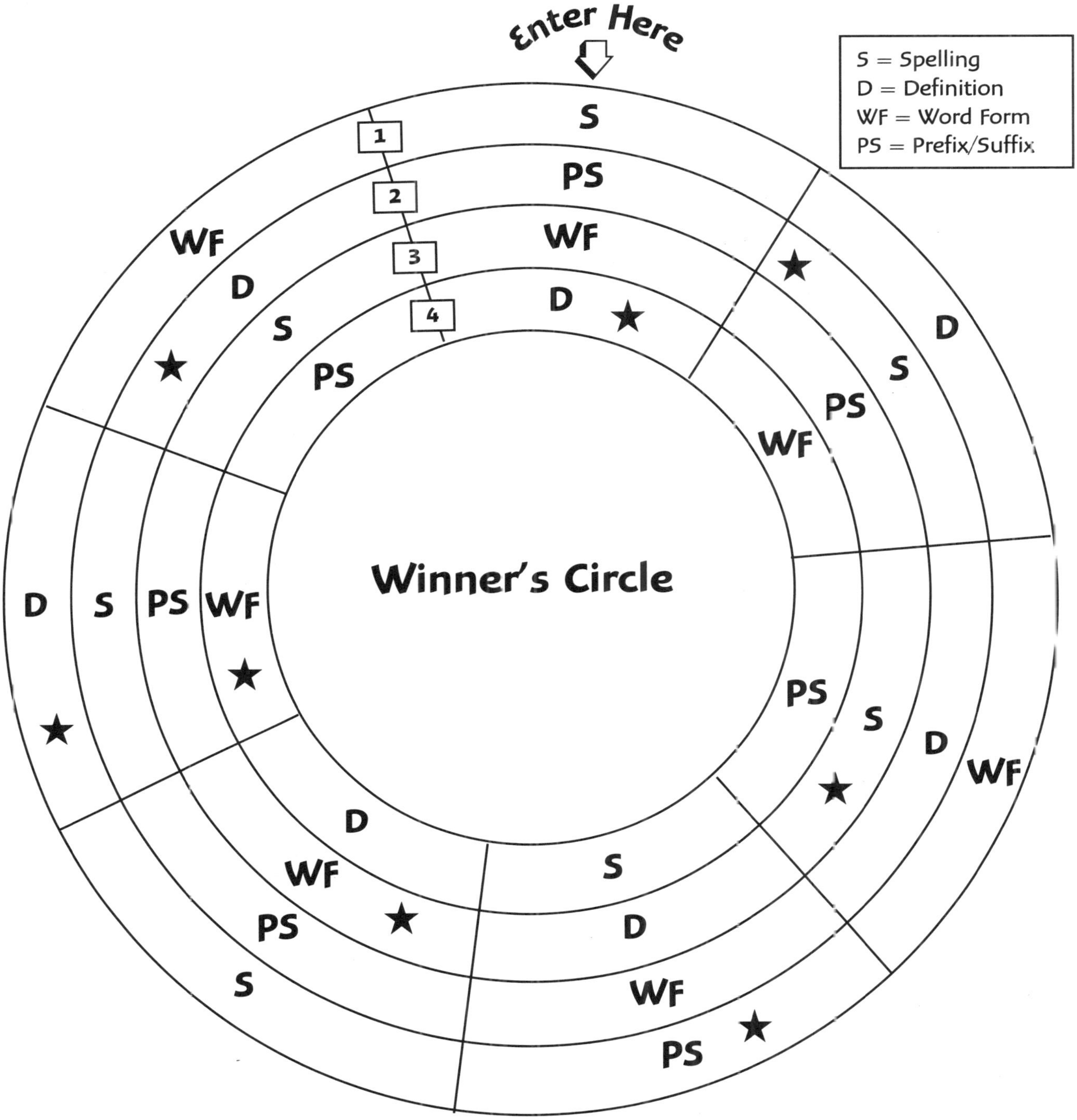

Place Spelling Cards face down here	Place Word Form Cards face down here	Place Prefix/Suffix Cards face down here	Place Definition Cards face down here

Photocopiable

Lexical Ladder – Game Board 2

11.2

S = Spelling
D = Definition
WF = Word Form
PS = Prefix/Suffix

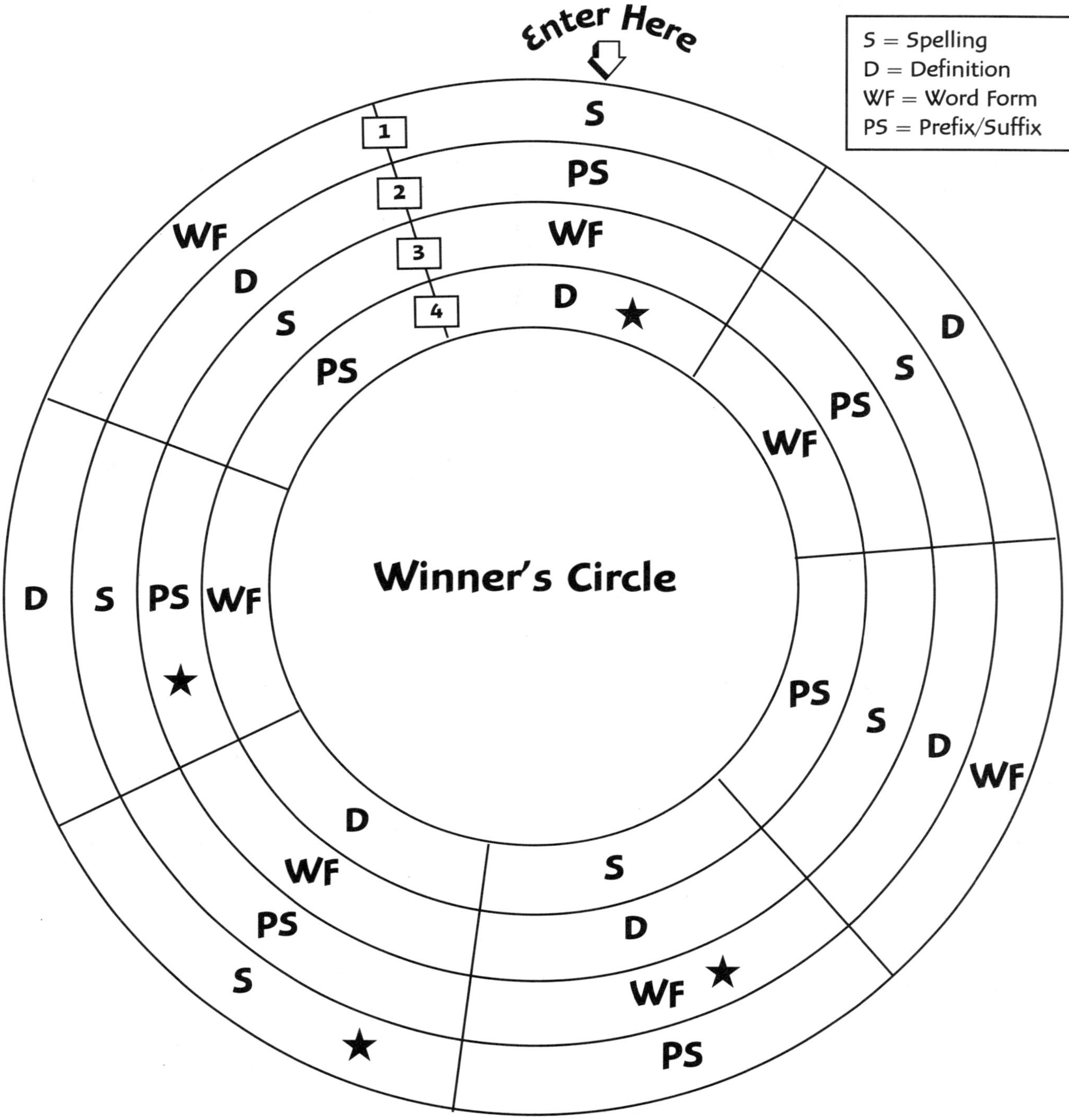

Enter Here

Winner's Circle

Place Spelling Cards face down here

Place Word Form Cards face down here

Place Prefix/Suffix Cards face down here

Place Definition Cards face down here

Photocopiable

Lexical Ladder – Spelling Cards

1) beautiful 2) absence 3) jealousy 4) fictitious	1) famous 2) judgment 3) accountant 4) accuracy	1) nephew 2) skiing 3) ambassador 4) carbohydrates	1) niece 2) sincerely 3) essential 4) accommodation
1) second 2) grammar 3) occasionally 4) technique	1) difficult 2) dangerous 3) discussion 4) extraordinary	1) necessary 2) decision 3) athlete 4) appreciate	1) allow 2) bicycle 3) beginning 4) disappointment
1) aunt 2) breathe 3) headache 4) courteous	1) finally 2) biggest 3) achieve 4) appreciate	1) million 2) embarrass 3) schedule 4) miscellaneous	1) special 2) occurrence 3) environment 4) dissatisfied
1) dessert 2) muscle 3) knowledge 4) foreign	1) first 2) doubt 3) disappear 4) possess	1) importance 2) disease 3) acceptable 4) accidentally	1) believe 2) attendance 3) fortunately 4) awkward

Photocopiable

Lexical Ladder – Definition Cards

1. final (adj) = last 2. theory (n) = a reasonable idea that hasn't been proven 3. policy (n) = an official way of doing something; a rule 4. legislation (n) = a law or set of laws	1. major (adj) = most important or largest 2. benefit (n) = something that is helpful 3. concept (n) = an idea or abstract thought 4. consistent (adj) = predictable and unchanging	1. per cent (n) = number in each 100 2. source (n) = the origin or starting point 3. context (n) = the situation (or circumstances) surrounding something 4. derived (adj) = coming from something else	1. occur (v) = to take place; happen 2. instance (n) = moment 3. issue (n) = something to be discussed (usually a problem) 4. significant (adj) = important
1. response (n) = answer 2. resident (n) = someone who lives in a place 3. established (adj) = well known or proven 4. analysis (n) = thinking about/looking carefully at something	1. create (v) = to make something new 2. appropriate (adj) = suitable 3. assume (v) = to believe something is true without confirmation 4. sector (n) = a part of a specific system or society	1. data (n) = factual information 2. corporate (adj) = related to business 3. authority (n) = person or ruling party in control 4. identified (adj) = found and categorized; named	1. available (adj) = not busy; able do something 2. demonstrate (v) = to show how to do something 3. assistance (n) = help 4. acquisition (n) = something that was got from elsewhere
1. required (adj) = needed 2. consent (v) = to agree 3. relevant (adj) = related to the topic being discussed 4. affect (v) = to do something to cause a change in something or someone	1. process (n) = something done step by step 2. techniques (n) = ways of doing something 3. elements (n) = parts of something 4. distinction (n) = a difference between things	1. period (n) = length of time 2. volume (n) = the amount of something; amount of noise 3. injury (n) = harm or damage 4. potential (adj) = possible	1. similar (adj) = alike 2. sequence (n) = a series or order of things 3. focus (v) = to bring into view; to give special attention 4. restricted (adj) = not open to everyone; open to specific group
1. legal (adj) = accepted by the law or government 2. complex (adj) = having many parts; difficult 3. regulations (n) = official rules 4. constraints (n) = restrictions; things that make something difficult to do	1. achieve (v) = to finish or do what you want 2. reaction (n) = something that happens as a result of another event 3. alternative (adj) = different 4. scheme (n) = plan	1. design (v) = to make a drawing or plan 2. published (adj) = printed in a book, magazine or newspaper 3. sufficient (adj) = enough 4. excluded (adj) = not a part of	1. previous (adj) = coming before 2. status (n) = rank; position in society 3. registered (adj) = listed with an official organization 4. sought (adj) = looked for

Photocopiable

Lexical Ladder – Word Form Cards

1. ambition = noun 2. per cent = noun 3. accurate = adjective 4. access = noun and verb	1. ability = noun 2. once = adverb 3. pursue = verb 4. quarrel = noun and verb	1. relevant = adjective 2. remain = verb 3. retained = adjective 4. scheme = noun and verb	1. obviously = adverb 2. work = noun and verb 3. lodging = noun 4. complex = noun and adjective
1. several = adjective 2. prevent = verb 3. idle = adjective 4. public = noun and adjective	1. miserable = adjective 2. multiply = verb 3. climate = noun 4. powder = noun and verb	1. respectful = adjective 2. light = noun and verb 3. confess = verb 4. boast = verb	1. available = adjective 2. equivalent = noun and adjective 3. entity = noun 4. empty = verb and adjective
1. opinion = noun 2. promise = noun and verb 3. prior = adjective 4. hence = adverb	1. individually = adverb 2. feather = noun 3. general = noun and adjective 4. secure = verb and adjective	1. valuable = adjective 2. help = noun and verb 3. parallel = adjective 4. imply = verb	1. permanent = adjective 2. positive = adjective 3. impose = verb 4. aware = adjective
1. define = verb 2. hypothesis = noun 3. process = noun and verb 4. journey = noun and verb	1. original = adjective 2. sudden = adjective 3. retire = verb 4. revenue = noun	1. implementation = noun 2. inquiry = noun 3. constraints = noun 4. glimpse = noun and verb	1. nature = noun 2. precious = adjective 3. maximum = noun and adjective 4. mercy = noun

Photocopiable

Lexical Ladder – Prefix/Suffix Cards

Card 1
1. What's the opposite of **careful**? Answer: careless
2. What prefix means **two**? Answer: bi-
3. What prefix means **half**? Answer: semi-
4. Change **child** into an adjective. Answer: childish

Card 2
1. What's the opposite of **useless**? Answer: useful
2. What prefix means **again**? Answer: re-
3. What prefix means **under**? Answer: sub-
4. Change **poet** into an adjective. Answer: poetic

Card 3
1. What's the opposite of **import**? Answer: export
2. What prefix means **before**? Answer: pre-
3. What prefix means **across**? Answer: trans-
4. Change **music** into an adjective. Answer: musical

Card 4
1. What's the opposite of **agree**? Answer: disagree
2. What prefix means **after**? Answer: post-
3. What prefix means **at a distance**? Answer: tele-
4. Change **agree** into an adjective. Answer: agreeable

Card 5
1. What's the opposite of **legal**? Answer: illegal
2. What does the prefix **mis-** mean? Answer: wrong, wrongly
3. What part of speech does **-ism** make? Answer: noun
4. Change **discuss** into a noun. Answer: discussion

Card 6
1. What's the opposite of **disappear**? Answer: appear
2. What does the prefix **un-** mean? Answer: not
3. What part of speech does **able** make? Answer: adjective
4. What does **television** mean? Answer: see from a distance

Card 7
1. What's the superlative of **weaker**? Answer: weakest
2. What does the prefix **uni-** mean? Answer: one (mono)
3. What part of speech does **-ity** make? Answer: noun
4. What does **bicycle** mean? Answer: 2 wheels

Card 8
1. What's the superlative of **strong**? Answer: strongest
2. What does the prefix **com-** mean? Answer: together
3. What part of speech does **-ous** make? Answer: adjective
4. What does **international** mean? Answer: between countries

---

Card 9
1. What prefix do most adverbs have? Answer: -ly
2. Change **importance** into an adjective. Answer: important
3. What does **replay** mean? Answer: play again
4. What does **extraterrestrial** mean? Answer: outside this land

Card 10
1. What's the opposite of **misbehave**? Answer: behave
2. Change **dangerous** into a noun. Answer: danger
3. What does **sub-zero** mean? Answer: below 0
4. What parts of speech often end with **-ent**? Answer: nouns and adjectives

Card 11
1. What's the opposite of **acceptable**? Answer: unacceptable
2. What's the person who plays a piano called? Answer: pianist
3. What does **misspell** mean? Answer: spell wrongly
4. What does **intra-** mean? Answer: within

Card 12
1. What does the prefix **non-** mean? Answer: not
2. Change **government** into a verb. Answer: govern
3. What does **post-game** mean? Answer: after game
4. What does **trans-** mean? Answer: across or change

Card 13
1. Change **teacher** into a verb. Answer: teach
2. What does the suffix **-ism** mean? Answer: idea
3. What does **audio-** mean? Answer: sound
4. What does the prefix **ambi-** mean? Answer: both

Card 14
1. Change **electrician** into an adjective. Answer: electric
2. What does **-ology** mean? Answer: study
3. What does **hydro-** mean? Answer: water
4. What does **-ician** mean? Answer: expert

Card 15
1. Change **goodness** into an adjective? Answer: good
2. What does **-ist** mean? Answer: someone who does
3. What does **-graph** mean? Answer: writing
4. What does **-itis** mean? Answer: inflammation

Card 16
1. What's the comparative of **big**? Answer: bigger
2. What does **anti-** mean? Answer: against
3. What does **-less** mean? Answer: without something
4. What does **peri-** mean? Answer: around

Photocopiable

Verbal Baseball

Game
12

Learning objective: To display knowledge of words (spelling, meaning, part of speech and possible prefix/suffix).

Game objective: To be the team with the highest score at the end of nine 'innings' (sets of team turns).

Organization: Played in small groups.

Preparation: Provide a Game Board, a set of vocabulary cards and a die for each group of students. Provide a place marker for each team (there are two teams in each group).

Description of the game:
1. The game is played according to the basic rules of baseball. There are two teams of players and each team can play until they receive three 'outs' (either because they have thrown a six, because they answer a question incorrectly when a player is 'at bat', or because a student receives assistance from a member of his/her team). There are nine innings (or sets of team turns) in the game.
2. Sit in teams with a Game Board in the middle.
3. Decide the order in which the players of your team will take turns.
4. The player who is taking the first turn (the 'batter') decides the level of question he or she would like to answer – the questions increase in level of difficulty, with a corresponding increase in the distance travelled around the baseball diamond. The player can choose a 'single', 'double', 'triple' or 'home run'.
5. The player throws a die to determine the type of question that will be asked: 1 = definition; 2 = spelling; 3 = part of speech; 4 = prefix/suffix; 5 = a 'walk' (the player moves to first base without answering a question and the next player in that team has a turn); 6 = a 'strikeout' (the player is out and the next player in that team comes to bat or the innings is over).
6. A member of the opposing team (the 'pitcher') draws a card of the appropriate type and asks the question at the level chosen by the student whose turn it is (the 'batter'): 1 = single; 2 = double; 3 = triple; 4 = home run.
7. If the answer is correct, the student's marker moves to the correct base. Any markers in front of that player move ahead accordingly and any that cross the home plate are recorded as runs.
8. After three 'outs' are recorded, it is the other team's turn 'at bat'.
9. Move your markers around the board as questions are asked and answered. There can only be one marker on a base at one time. Record the score at the bottom of the playing board.
10. Play continues until nine innings have been played. The winning team is the one with the highest score.

Variations:
- Limit the number of innings to suit the time required or the interest level and vocabulary production of your students.
- Play the game with a 'one strike, you're out' rule.
- Play as a whole class using an overhead transparency.
- Use the cards from Lexical Ladder on pages 63–66.

Verbal Baseball – Game Board

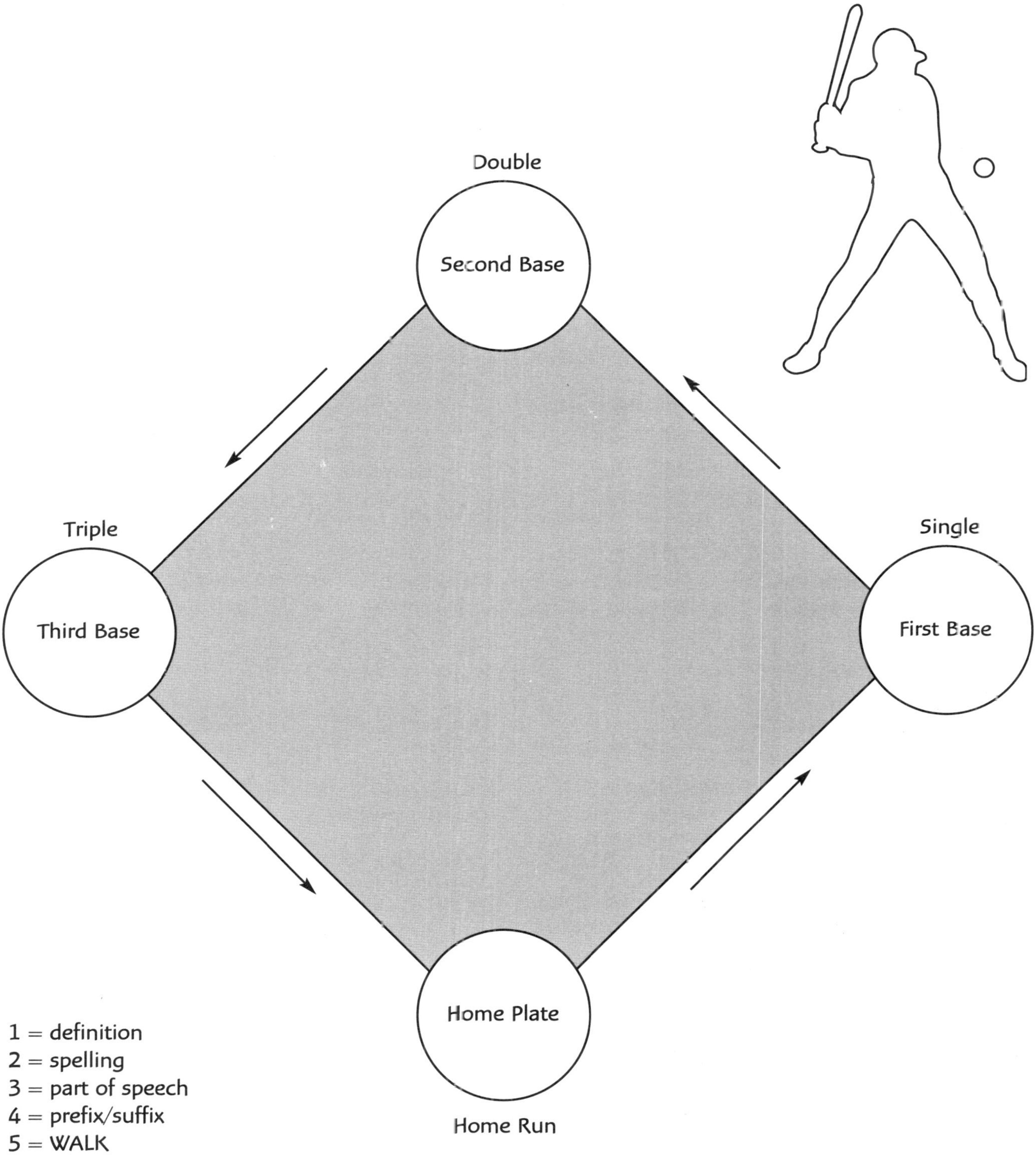

Double
Second Base

Triple
Third Base

Single
First Base

Home Plate
Home Run

1 = definition
2 = spelling
3 = part of speech
4 = prefix/suffix
5 = WALK
6 = STRIKEOUT

Team	1	2	3	4	5	6	7	8	9	Total

Photocopiable

Verbal Baseball – Definition Cards

---

1. select (v) = to choose
2. series (n) = a group of things that come one after another
3. shift (v) = to move
4. reliance (n) = state of being dependent on something

---

1. text (n) = written material
2. internal (adj) = found inside
3. circumstances (n) = factors that affect a situation
4. considerable (adj) = large or important

---

1. positive (adj) = happy; considering the good things (not negative)
2. attitude (n) = the way a person feels or thinks about something
3. constant (adj) = not changing
4. ensure (v) = to make sure

---

1. normal (adj) = average; like others
2. apparent (adj) = easy to see
3. imply (v) = to make understood without saying directly
4. emphasis (n) = stress or importance put on something

---

1. conclusion (n) = the end
2. despite (prep) = regardless; without caring about something
3. corresponding (adj) = matching; similar
4. criteria (n) = standards used to judge something

---

1. purchase (v) = to buy
2. domestic (adj) = related to the home; not wild
3. conference (n) = a large formal meeting
4. access (n) = ability, right or chance to use something ; (v) = to find and use something

---

1. security (n) = the state of being safe
2. hypothesis (n) = theory; unproven idea about something
3. prior (adj) = coming before
4. parameters (n) = limits that control how something can be done

---

1. traditional (adj) = following ideals from the past
2. obvious (adj) = easy to see or understand
3. impose (v) = to force something upon people
4. regime (n) = a ruling party or government

---

1. physical (adj) = related to the body
2. alter (v) = to change
3. subsequent (adj) = following
4. implementation (n) = the process of making a plan happen

---

1. initial (adj) = the first
2. option (n) = a choice
3. hence (adv) = therefore; for this reason
4. implications (n) = things you don't say directly but hope others will understand; possible effects

---

1. negative (adj) = seeing things badly; (not positive)
2. academic (adj) = related to studying
3. aware (adj) = knowing something is true or exists
4. retained (adj) = kept back

---

1. maximum (n) = the largest amount needed or possible
2. parallel (adj) = lines running next to each other but always at the same distance apart
3. adequate (adj) = sufficient; enough
4. amendment (n) = a change

---

1. summary (adj) = a short version
2. conflict (n) = a disagreement
3. evolution (n) = slow change over time
4. entity (n) = something that exists as a single, separate and complete unit

---

1. error (n) = mistake
2. psychology (n) = study of the mind
3. substitution (n) = something used instead of something else
4. pursue (v) = to chase or look for

---

1. goals (n) = things you want to do
2. equivalent (n) = something of equal value
3. adjustment (n) = change
4. revenue (n) = money earned by a business

---

1. energy (n) = ability to do a lot of work; power
2. external (adj) = on the outside
3. enable (v) = to allow someone to do something
4. enforce (v) = make people follow a rule or law

Photocopiable

Verbal Baseball – Spelling Cards

1) language 2) occupation 3) opposite 4) consonant	1) yesterday 2) medicine 3) geography 4) tongue	1) breakfast 2) intelligent 3) vowel 4) recognize	1) thirsty 2) village 3) preference 4) humorous
1) expensive 2) sauce 3) dynamite 4) obedience	1) awful 2) escape 3) yield 4) villain	1) polite 2) combination 3) straight 4) affordable	1) comfortable 2) obvious 3) literature 4) persuade
1) tomorrow 2) moral 3) political 4) distinguish	1) hobbies 2) separate 3) recommend 4) frequency	1) husband 2) variety 3) particularly 4) succeed	1) wife 2) previous 3) evaluate 4) reliable
1) education 2) available 3) ancient 4) preference	1) science 2) particularly 3) prospective 4) qualifications	1) chemistry 2) security 3) advertisement 4) exhausted	1) favourite 2) satisfaction 3) managerial 4) consumption

Photocopiable

Verbal Baseball – Parts of Speech Cards

Card 1
1. acceptable = adjective
2. occur = verb
3. male = adjective and noun
4. affect = verb

Card 2
1. decisively = adverb
2. absence = noun
3. descend = verb
4. assume = verb

Card 3
1. particular = adjective
2. jealous = adjective
3. area = noun
4. quarrel = noun and verb

Card 4
1. naturally = adverb
2. mystery = noun
3. recent = adjective
4. liquid = noun and adjective

Card 5
1. loyal = adjective
2. achieve = verb
3. cruel = adjective
4. challenge = noun and verb

Card 6
1. imagine = verb
2. loss = noun
3. volume = noun
4. focus = noun and verb

Card 7
1. actually = adverb
2. humble = adjective
3. established = adjective
4. firm = noun and adjective

Card 8
1. razor = noun
2. arise = verb
3. concept = adjective
4. coarse = adjective

Card 9
1. ensure = verb
2. guess = noun and verb
3. urge = verb
4. elastic = noun and adjective

Card 10
1. amendment = noun
2. mercy = noun
3. recognize = verb
4. issue = noun or verb

Card 11
1. modern = adjective
2. sympathy = noun
3. status = noun
4. tame = verb and adjective

Card 12
1. topic = noun
2. client = noun
3. trade = noun and verb
4. awkward = adjective

Card 13
1. insect = noun
2. category = noun
3. sought = adjective
4. consent = noun and verb

Card 14
1. error = noun
2. despite = preposition
3. evil = noun and adjective
4. exact = adjective

Card 15
1. injury = noun
2. alter = verb
3. offer = noun and verb
4. evaluate = verb

Card 16
1. basically = adverb
2. evidence = noun
3. design = noun and verb
4. form = noun and verb

Verbal Baseball – Prefix/Suffix Cards

Card 1
1. What's the suffix in **friendship**? Answer: ship
2. Change **allowance** into a verb. Answer: allow
3. Is a book **boring** or **bored**? Answer: boring
4. What does **-ium** mean? Answer: place where

Card 2
1. What's the suffix in **beggar**? Answer: -ar
2. What's the base noun in **homeless**? Answer: home
3. Change **pleasant** into a verb. Answer: please
4. What does **geo-** mean? Answer: Earth

Card 3
1. What's the suffix in **neighbourhood**? Answer: hood
2. What's the suffix in **cloudy**? Answer: -y
3. Change **president** into a verb. Answer: preside
4. What does **-log** mean? Answer: about words

Card 4
1. What's the suffix in **reddish**? Answer: ish
2. Change **glorious** into a noun. Answer: glory
3. Change **dependence** into a verb. Answer: depend
4. What does **-proof** mean? Answer: not allowing in

Card 5
1. What's the opposite of **available**? Answer: unavailable
2. What's the opposite of **artful**? Answer: artless
3. What prefix means **by yourself**? Answer: auto-
4. What does **thermo-** mean? Answer: heat

Card 6
1. What's the opposite of **advantage**? Answer: disadvantage
2. What does the prefix **tri-** mean? Answer: three
3. Which prefix means **many**? Answer: poly-; multi-
4. What does **geology** mean? Answer: study of the Earth

Card 7
1. What's the opposite of **unskilled**? Answer: skilled
2. What does the prefix **dis-** mean? Answer: not; opposite
3. What does the prefix **sym-** mean? Answer: with; together
4. What does **autobiography** mean? Answer: book about your own life

Card 8
1. What's the opposite of **prove**? Answer: disprove
2. What does the prefix **semi-** mean? Answer: half
3. What part of speech is made from the suffix **-cy**? Answer: nouns
4. What does **soundproof** mean? Answer: sound cannot get through

---

Card 9
1. What's the opposite of **complete**? Answer: incomplete
2. Change **different** into a noun. Answer: difference
3. What does the suffix **-or** mean? Answer: someone who does something
4. What does **theo-** mean? Answer: about God

Card 10
1. What's the opposite of **honest**? Answer: dishonest
2. Change **dependable** into a verb Answer: depend
3. Change **allowance** into a verb. Answer: allow
4. What does **telephone** mean? Answer: sound from a distance

Card 11
1. What's the opposite of **breakable**? Answer: unbreakable
2. Change **weak** into a noun. Answer: weakness
3. What does the prefix **co-** mean? Answer: together
4. Change **modern** into a verb. Answer: modernize

Card 12
1. What's the superlative of **hot**? Answer: hottest
2. Change **creative** into a verb. Answer: create
3. What does the prefix **counter-** mean? Answer: opposite
4. Change **fury** into an adjective. Answer: furious

Card 13
1. Which part of speech usually ends in **-ly**? Answer: adverb
2. What's the opposite of **rational**? Answer: irrational
3. Change **distant** into a noun. Answer: distance
4. What two parts of speech end in **-ant**? Answer: nouns and adjectives

Card 14
1. What part of speech usually ends in **-est**? Answer: adjective
2. What does **ex-** mean? Answer: no longer
3. Change **soft** into a noun. Answer: softness
4. What does **wooden** mean? Answer: made of wood

Card 15
1. What's the opposite of **harmful**? Answer: harmless
2. What does **triangle** mean? Answer: 3 angles.
3. Change **management** into a verb. Answer: manage
4. What does **ultra-** mean? Answer: extreme, beyond

Card 16
1. What's the suffix in the word **endless**? Answer: less
2. What's the opposite of **logical**? Answer: illogical
3. Change **direction** into a verb. Answer: direct
4. What does **ecology** mean? Answer: study of the environment

---

Photocopiable

Jigsaw Joinings

Game 13

Learning objective: To display knowledge of word relationships by correctly identifying the link between two given words on the game board.

Game objective: To be the team with the highest number of identified 'joinings' (i.e., relationships) at the end of the game.

Organization: Played in groups.

Preparation: Provide a Game Board and two coloured pencils for each group.

Description of the game:
1. Groups play in two teams. The teams sit facing each other with the Game Board in the middle, so it can be turned towards the team currently in control of the game.
2. Students decide which team will go first.
3. In turn, each team selects a pair of connecting words on the Game Board.
4. The team then describes the relationship they see between those two words – perhaps they are synonyms, antonyms, begin with the same letter, the same parts of speech or members of the same word family.
   Note: Sometimes there is more than one correct answer, e.g., the words may be part of the same word family and also begin with the same letter.
5. If the students from the first team are correct, they get one point and they colour in the connecting area between the two words (i.e., the tab on the jigsaw piece). If they are incorrect, they do not get any points and they do not colour the area between the words.
6. The other team then select their words and describe the relationship. Teams have only one guess on each turn.
7. Play continues until a valid relationship has been identified for each pair of connecting words, the time allowed has expired, or no further relationships can be identified.

Variations:
- This can be played as a whole class on an overhead transparency.
- A blank template can be used, with the teams taking turns writing words in connecting spaces and stating the relationship they have shown (e.g., the second word is the same part of speech or starts with the same letter).

Jigsaw Joinings – Game Board

Photocopiable

Jigsaw Joinings – Relationship Answers

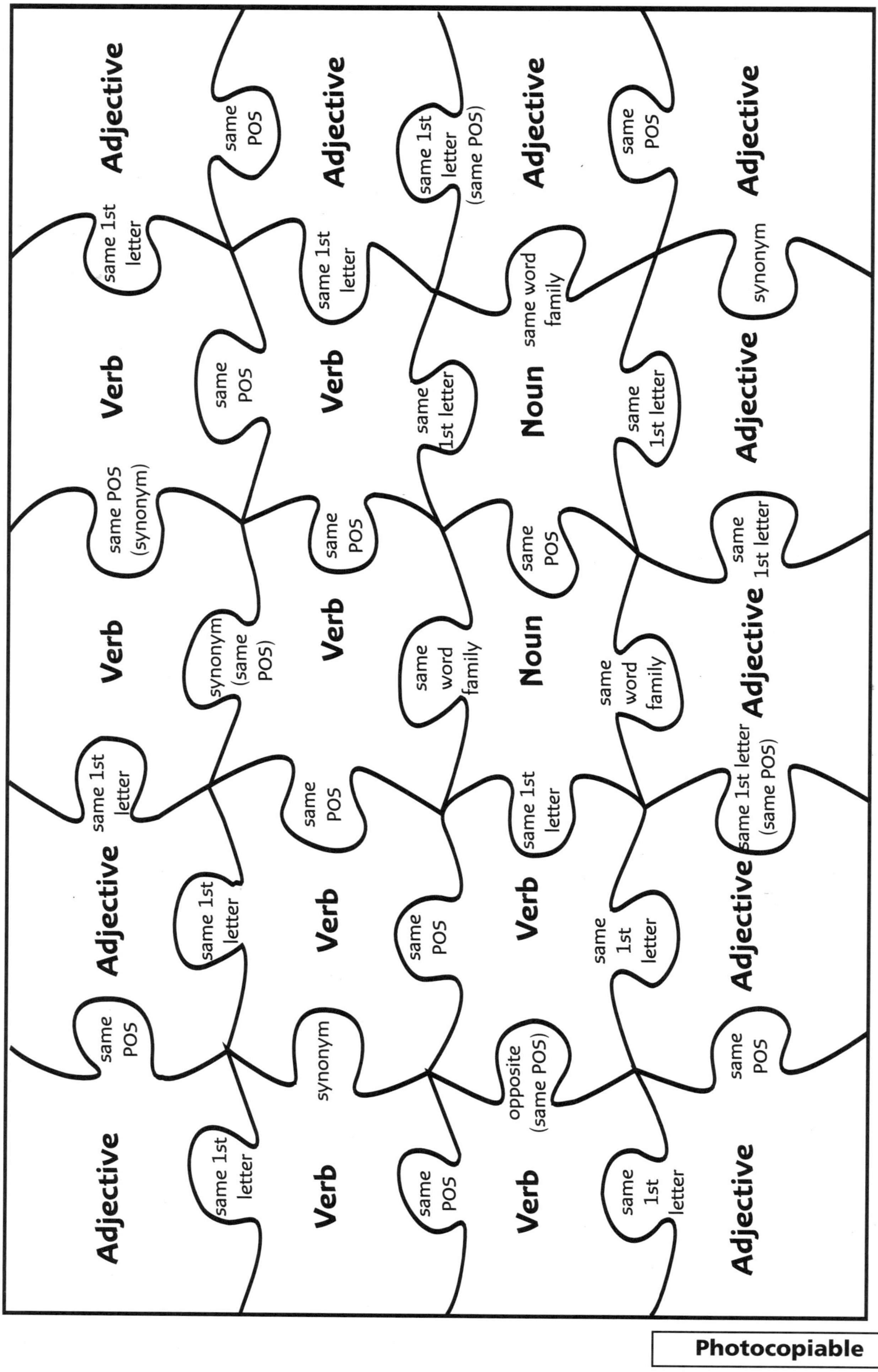

Jigsaw Joinings – Template 1

Photocopiable

Jigsaw Joinings – Template 2

13.4

Photocopiable

POS Placement

Game 14

Learning objective: To practise identifying parts of speech.

Game objective: To place word cards in the proper spaces in order to move to the opposite side of the board, leaving as many word cards on the board as possible (as in the game, *Checkers*).

Organization: Played in pairs or teams of 2 students.

Preparation:
Note: There are two forms of the game: one requires the students to play with set word cards (POS Placement 1) and the other requires them to identify the parts of speech of words that are already printed on the board (POS Placement 2).
1. Copy one Game Board for each pair or group of students.
2. If playing POS Placement 1, provide a full set of word cards for each team (each set printed in a different colour).

Description of the game:
1. The pairs or teams sit with the Game Board in the middle. The students decide which team will play on the shaded squares and which will play on the white ones.
2. In turn, a student from each team chooses one of its squares, beginning on the closest row. (When the playable squares closest to the team are full, cards may be added to the next row, and so on.)
3. After choosing a square, the student selects a word card that matches the part of speech on the square and places it on the board (e.g., he/she places *careful* on an *adjective* square).
4. If the students are playing **POS Placement 2**, the rules are the same.
5. The teacher acts as moderator, if necessary.
6. If the word is correct, the player takes another turn. The maximum number of consecutive turns is two.
7. If the word is incorrect, the player removes the word card and play passes to the other team.
8. If a team's word card is beside one of the opposing team's word cards, on their turn they can remove the opposing team's card by 'jumping over' it (i.e., by placing their next card on the other side of their opponent's word card and then removing the opponent's card). Spaces cleared by 'jumping' in this way can be filled in later play.
9. Play continues until one team has placed as many of their word cards as possible on the board. The team with the most word cards on the board is the winner.

Variations:
- Have students make sentences with the words when they place them on the board.
- Students write their own example of the part of speech listed on the board in order to move across the board.
- Use the blank checkerboard template on page 85 to practise any particular part of speech you choose.

POS Placement 1 – Game Board

adjective	noun	verb	adverb	adverb	verb	noun	adjective
noun	verb	adverb	adjective	adjective	adverb	verb	noun
verb	adverb	adjective	noun	noun	adjective	adverb	verb
adverb	adjective	noun	verb	verb	noun	adjective	adverb
adjective	noun	verb	adverb	adverb	verb	noun	adjective
noun	verb	adverb	adjective	adjective	adverb	verb	noun
verb	adverb	adjective	noun	noun	adjective	adverb	verb
adverb	adjective	noun	verb	verb	noun	adjective	adverb

Photocopiable

POS Placement 1 – Word Cards

14.2

careful	device	cut	usually	actually	produce	politics	useful
basis	achieve	recently	athletic	confused	sincerely	create	employment
discuss	never	young	doubt	inventor	separate	finally	appreciate
seriously	straight	disease	move	descend	version	reliable	easily
foreign	knowledge	balance	annually	simply	improve	discipline	apparent
biology	know	also	supportive	sick	instead	want	vengeance
breathe	definitely	special	fiction	facility	guilty	besides	open
primarily	constant	event	fly	track	tension	workable	sometimes

Photocopiable

POS Placement 2 – Game Board

careful	device	cut	usually	actually	produce	politics	useful
basis	achieve	recently	athletic	confused	sincerely	create	employment
discuss	never	young	doubt	inventor	separate	finally	appreciate
seriously	straight	disease	move	descend	version	reliable	easily
foreign	knowledge	balance	annually	simply	improve	discipline	apparent
biology	know	also	supportive	sick	instead	want	vengeance
breathe	definitely	special	fiction	facility	guilty	besides	open
primarily	constant	event	fly	track	tension	workable	sometimes

Photocopiable

POS Placement 2 – Answers

adjective	noun	verb or noun	adverb	adverb	verb or noun	noun	adjective
noun	verb	adverb	adjective	adjective	adverb	verb	noun
verb	adverb	adjective	noun or verb	noun	adjective or verb	adverb	verb
adverb	adjective	noun	verb or noun	verb	noun	adjective	adverb
adjective	noun	verb or noun	adverb	adverb	verb	noun	adjective
noun	verb	adverb	adjective	adjective	adverb	verb	noun
verb	adverb	adjective	noun	noun	adjective	adverb	verb or adjective
adverb	adjective	noun	verb	verb or noun	noun	adjective	adverb

Photocopiable

POS Placement – Template

Parts of Speech Journey

Game

Learning objective: To recognize parts of speech and practise giving definitions of words.

Game objective: To move around the board by correctly identifying parts of speech. To be the first player to reach the end of the board by defining words correctly.

Organization: Played in small groups of 3–5 students.

Preparation:
1. Copy one Game Board for each group.
2. Make a set of parts of speech cards for each group.
3. Provide a place marker for each student.

Optional: Make a set of special command cards for each group. See the 'Optional' section in the Description of the game.

Description of the game:
1. Students shuffle the cards and place them face down in the 'new cards' box.
2. In turn, each student draws a card and moves his/her place marker to the first space that contains a word with the same part of speech as the card (e.g., if a student draws *verb*, he/she must move to the next space with a verb on it). If a player skips the correct part of speech and another student catches the player, the player must return to start. **Note:** some words have more than one part of speech.
3. After the student has moved to a space with the correct part of speech, he/she must define the word on that space. If the student gives a correct definition, the student stays where he/she is. If the student gives an incorrect definition and the other students catch him/her, the student must go back to a previous word that is the same part of speech.
4. No definitions or parts of speech are provided. The other students judge if the player is correct. This tests the vocabulary knowledge of the other students as well as the player. The teacher acts as moderator if problems arise.
5. After giving a definition for one word, the student places the used card face up in the 'used card' box.
6. Repeat Steps 1–5 for each student. The first student to reach the Finish box wins.

Optional: Add the Special Command Cards. If you include these cards in the game, the students must do as they are told. There are extra penalty cards which instruct students to go back, or to send another student back to Start. There are move ahead cards that tell a player how many spaces to move ahead, regardless of part of speech. There are also move ahead cards that tell a student to move ahead of two nouns, verbs or adjectives.

Variation:
- Write words from your course on the blank board template on page 90.

Parts of Speech Journey – Game Board

15.1

	Place new cards face down here				Place used cards face up here			START
	reliably	debate	invent		powder	expertly	conclusive	general
	ground		original		male		topic	pause
	expensive		rapidly		process		known	remind
	committee		variety		complex		aim	flexible
	intelligent		predict		regularly		elastic	secure
	probable		exact		explorer		focus	challenge
	research		constantly		honest		apparent	key
cruel			chart		offer		form	publish
FINISH	prevent	energy		globally		previously	achievable	naturally

Photocopiable

Parts of Speech Journey – POS Cards

noun	verb	adjective	adverb
noun	verb	adjective	adverb
noun	verb	adjective	adverb
noun	verb	adjective	adverb
noun	verb	adjective	adverb
noun	verb	adjective	adverb
noun	verb	adjective	adverb
noun	verb	adjective	adverb
noun	verb	adjective	adverb
noun	verb	adjective	noun
noun	verb	adjective	verb
noun	verb	adjective	adjective

Photocopiable

Parts of Speech Journey – Special Command Cards

Move ahead 2 nouns	Move ahead 2 verbs	Move ahead 2 adjectives	Move ahead 5 spaces
Move ahead 2 nouns	Move ahead 2 verbs	Move ahead 2 adjectives	Move ahead 5 spaces
Move ahead 3 spaces	Move ahead 3 spaces	Move ahead 4 spaces	Move ahead 2 spaces
Send someone to Start	Send someone to Start	Send someone to Start	Send someone to Start
Go back 2 spaces	Go back 2 spaces	Go back 3 spaces	Go back 5 spaces
Go back to Start	Go back to Start	Go back to Start	Go back to Start

Parts of Speech Journey – Template

Place used cards face up here

Place new cards face down here

FINISH

START

Photocopiable

Close Call

Game

Learning objective: To get across meanings of words by providing definitions and examples and to recall vocabulary words by category.

Game objective: To be the team to win the most points by working out words described by one team member.

Organization: Played as a whole class.

Preparation:
1. Copy a set of category cards.
2. Provide a timer or watch or clock with a second hand for the class.

Description of Activity:
1. Divide the class into two or more teams.
2. One student from Team A comes to the front of the classroom and is given a category card at random. The teacher or a student reads aloud the title of the category, but not the words on the card.
3. The student at the front of the class describes the words on the card one by one. He/she may not say the words aloud in whole or part (so a description of *blackboard* cannot include the words *black* or *board*). The teacher should monitor the game and give an agreed signal if the student says one of the words (or part of a word), for example, ringing a bell. In this case, the team does not win the point and the student may not try to describe that word again.
4. Students from Team A shout out the words as they guess them. When a student on Team A says the correct answer, the team wins one point.
5. If the team guesses all the words on the card before the time is finished, they win two bonus points.
6. Simultaneously, another team watches the time and stops the play after a minute.
7. It is then Team B's turn. Repeat steps 2–6 for each of the teams. Every student should come to the front of the class at least once.

Variations:
- Decide if communication using body language is permitted. If it is not, have the student who is giving the definitions hold a pencil with both hands to stop him/her from gesturing.
- Determine if students must describe the words on the Category Card in the order they appear on the card or whether the students can select words from the card at random. You can also give students the option to 'pass'– i.e., to just take part in guessing rather than describing.
- Give the category title only. The teams brainstorm words and write a list in one minute. Teams only get points for words that are on the card.

Close Call – Category Cards

Things in a kitchen	Things in a living room	Things in a bedroom	Things in a classroom
1. oven / stove	1. sofa	1. bed	1. black / white board
2. refrigerator	2. television	2. pillow	2. student desks
3. food	3. stereo	3. blanket	3. books
4. sink	4. coffee table	4. sheets	4. chairs
5. pots / pans	5. plants	5. chest of drawers	5. map
6. dishes / plates	6. lamp	6. wardrobe	6. books
7. knives	7. rug	7. night stand	7. overhead projector
8. cupboards	8. bookcase	8. reading lamp	8. television
9. table	9. armchair	9. mirror	9. CD /tape player
10. chairs	10. pictures	10. make-up table	10. posters

Sports with balls	Individual sports	Time words	Map words
1. football / soccer	1. swimming	1. minute	1. north
2. basketball	2. running	2. hour	2. east
3. tennis	3. skating	3. second	3. south
4. ping-pong / table tennis	4. weightlifting	4. clock	4. country
5. volleyball	5. gymnastics	5. watch	5. continent
6. golf	6. skiing	6. week	6. ocean
7. bowling	7. archery	7. day	7. river
8. lacrosse	8. surfing	8. month	8. province
9. rugby	9. cycling	9. year	9. legend / key
10. baseball	10. walking	10. night	10. mountain

Transportation	Women's clothing	Men's clothing	Electronics
1. car	1. blouse	1. tie	1. radio
2. bus	2. skirt	2. suit	2. television
3. train	3. dress	3. belt	3. computer
4. plane	4. nightgown	4. vest	4. DVD player
5. metro	5. high heels	5. overalls	5. mobile phone
6. ship / boat	6. pantyhose / tights	6. boots	6. beeper
7. helicopter	7. hat	7. jacket	7. computer
8. ferry	8. gloves	8. uniform	8. stereo
9. truck	9. cardigan	9. pyjamas	9. air-conditioner
10. bicycle	10. bra	10. boxer shorts	10. heater

Things in a book	Liquids	Jewellery	Make up
1. chapter	1. water	1. earrings	1. lipstick
2. index	2. petrol	2. necklace	2. eye shadow
3. page	3. juice	3. bracelet	3. mascara
4. table of contents	4. milk	4. watch	4. blush
5. paragraphs	5. oil	5. ring	5. powder
6. words	6. coffee	6. brooch / pin	6. eye liner
7. letters	7. tea	7. tie clip	7. nail polish
8. preface	8. cola	8. nose ring	8. lip liner
9. glossary	9. sauce	9. belly ring	9. foundation
10. epilogue	10. wine	10. pendant	10. moisturizer

Photocopiable

Close Call – Category Cards

Tools	Weather	Body parts in pairs	Face
1. hammer	1. rain	1. eyes	1. lips
2. nails	2. snow	2. ears	2. nose
3. wrench	3. sunny	3. hands	3. teeth
4. saw	4. cloudy	4. legs	4. eyes
5. pliers	5. fog	5. feet	5. eyebrows
6. tape measure	6. spring	6. arms	6. cheeks
7. screwdriver	7. summer	7. elbows	7. moustache
8. sander	8. temperature	8. shoulders	8. mouth
9. paint brush	9. wind	9. wrists	9. chin
10. drill	10. ice	10. ankles	10. beard

The car	Red things	White things	Question words
1. wheels	1. fire trucks	1. wedding dress	1. how
2. seat belt	2. stop signs	2. clouds	2. where
3. engine	3. heart	3. tennis dress	3. why
4. windshield	4. strawberries	4. golf balls	4. how old
5. brake	5. apples	5. snow	5. who
6. horn	6. roses	6. paper	6. which
7. stick shift / gear stick	7. blood	7. chalk	7. what
8. boot / trunk	8. ambulance lights	8. milk	8. when
9. steering wheel	9. cola cans	9. doves	9. how long
10. exhaust	10. lipstick	10. cauliflower	10. how many

Two-letter words	Three-letter words	Grammar	Teacher words
1. am	1. are	1. past tense	1. homework
2. it	2. one	2. full stop	2. sit down
3. on	3. let	3. verb	3. write
4. is	4. dog	4. infinitive	4. read
5. no	5. tea	5. future	5. listen
6. to	6. sit	6. present perfect	6. notes
7. an	7. new	7. plural	7. assignment
8. be	8. win	8. third person	8. worksheet
9. up	9. run	9. comma	9. pronounce
10. we	10. now	10. apostrophe	10. spell

Computer	Maths	Toys	Cooking
1. monitor	1. addition	1. ball	1. cut
2. mouse	2. subtraction	2. doll	2. bake
3. modem	3. multiply	3. blocks	3. stir
4. internet	4. division	4. stuffed animal	4. heat
5. icon	5. fraction	5. train	5. broil / boil
6. click	6. graph	6. teddy bear	6. chop
7. drive	7. percent	7. truck	7. slice
8. keyboard	8. negative	8. puzzle	8. fry
9. printer	9. positive	9. doll's house	9. whip
10. browser	10. solve	10. bike	10. blend

Photocopiable

Creative Categories

Game 17

Learning objective: To recall and generate words in categories.

Game objective: To be the team to win the most points by guessing words or phrases belonging to a category.

Organization: Played as a class.

Preparation:
1. Copy a set of category cards.
2. Provide a special card, block or object students can easily grab.

Description of the game:
1. Divide the class into two teams.
2. One student from each team comes to the front of the classroom. The two students stand facing each other with a special card, block or object placed on a table at an equal distance between them.
3. The teacher calls out a category name. The first student to think of a word he/she believes fits the category and grab the object gets a chance to say the word. For example, if the category is *vegetables* the student may guess *carrot*.
4. **Note**: The student has only 10 seconds to answer after grabbing the object. This prevents students from grabbing the object without having an answer.
5. If the word is on the category card, that team wins the play. No points are assigned. Go to Step 7.
6. If the word is *not* on the category card (even though it may be a word in the category), the other team's student has a chance to win the play for his/her team. He/she must guess a possible word in the same category in 15 seconds or less. If he/she is correct, the play goes to his/her team. If not, the play returns to the first team. 'The play' means that the team has a chance to guess all 7 words in the category.
7. Each player from the team that wins the play has one chance to guess a word or phrase in the category. He/she cannot get help from any other team member. If the answer is correct, the team wins a point. If the guess is not on the category card, the team earns one 'strike'.
8. If the team guesses all seven words before earning three strikes, repeat Steps 2–7 with a new student from each team coming forward.
9. If the team earns three strikes before guessing all seven words, the other team has a chance to 'steal' the play. They may guess words until they earn only one strike. For every word they guess correctly, they win a point. When they get a strike, repeat Steps 2–7 with a new student for each team coming to the front of the class.
10. The team with the most points wins.

Variations:
- You may recognize this game as *Family Feud*, the popular television show where the categories were made by surveys. Create your own surveys and develop your own category cards based on the top seven answers to survey questions.
- Use the category cards from Close Call (pages 93 and 94).

Creative Categories – Category Cards

Animals in a zoo 1. lion 2. monkey 3. elephant 4. bear 5. tiger 6. giraffe 7. zebra	**Animals on farms** 1. cow 2. chicken 3. duck 4. sheep 5. goat 6. dog 7. horse	**Animals as pets** 1. dog 2. cat 3. snake 4. turtle 5. fish 6. guinea pig 7. bird
Things in a lady's bag 1. lipstick 2. money 3. brush/comb 4. tissue 5. mirror 6. credit cards 7. pen	**Things in a briefcase** 1. files 2. pen 3. book 4. calculator 5. highlighter 6. portfolio 7. business cards	**Things in a school bag** 1. books 2. notebooks 3. pens 4. pencils 5. rubber 6. calculator 7. pencil sharpener
Things in the ocean 1. fish 2. octopus 3. whale 4. seal 5. seaweed 6. dolphin 7. clam	**Things you bring to the beach** 1. towel 2. swimsuit 3. umbrella 4. pail and shovel / bucket and spade 5. beach bag 6. suntan lotion 7. beach ball	**Things you keep in a closet / cupboard** 1. clothing 2. hangers 3. sports equipment 4. linens/sheets 5. shoes 6. jackets/coats 7. umbrellas
Gifts for men 1. tie 2. sweater 3. gloves 4. computer game 5. pen set 6. cologne 7. book	**Gifts for women** 1. jewellery 2. perfume 3. chocolate 4. flowers 5. something for the kitchen 6. slippers 7. gloves	**Things in an office** 1. files 2. fax 3. computers 4. telephone 5. desk 6. printers 7. copy machine

Photocopiable

Creative Categories – Category Cards

Things you do with your feet
1. dance
2. run
3. walk
4. march
5. jump
6. skip
7. kick

Things you do with your mouth
1. eat
2. talk
3. sing
4. drink
5. lick
6. whistle
7. kiss

Things you see in the sky
1. clouds
2. birds
3. sun
4. planes
5. balloons
6. butterflies
7. Superman

Things people do on weekends
1. sleep late
2. watch TV
3. go to dinner
4. run errands
5. chores
6. see friends
7. go to the movies

Vegetables
1. carrot
2. potato
3. spinach
4. broccoli
5. tomato
6. celery
7. pea

Fruits
1. apple
2. banana
3. grape
4. orange
5. strawberry
6. melon
7. pear

Reasons for being late
1. oversleep
2. miss the train
3. traffic jam
4. watch breaks
5. accident
6. have another appointment
7. forget

Outdoor jobs
1. gardener
2. pool cleaner
3. garbage collector
4. construction worker
5. bike messenger
6. postal carrier / postman
7. doorman

Hospital jobs
1. doctor
2. nurse
3. lab technician
4. file clerk
5. receptionist
6. surgeon
7. X-ray technician

Places in the airport
1. arrivals
2. departures
3. customs
4. baggage claim
5. duty free
6. ticket counter
7. information

Kinds of insect
1. ant
2. mosquito
3. fly
4. cockroach
5. cricket
6. butterfly
7. spider

Musical instruments
1. guitar
2. piano
3. drum
4. violin
5. trumpet / horn
6. organ
7. flute

Photocopiable

Word Search

Game 18

Learning objective: To practise word recognition and increase knowledge of common letter combinations by finding words in a letter grid.

Game objective: To be the group that finds the most words within the set time limit.

Organization: Played in teams of two or in small groups.

Preparation:
1. Provide one sheet of letters (either 12 x 12 or 8 x 8) for each group of students (or for each student – see Variations).
2. If desired, provide a timer for each group to control the duration of the game.

Description of the game:
1. Each group of students receives a letter grid. The students sit in a group looking at the grid.
2. The teacher determines the direction of play, depending on the level of the students. Words can be read a) only horizontally and vertically; b) with diagonals permitted as well, or c) in any direction in the grid.
3. The teacher starts the activity (or the students start the timer). The group work together to locate combinations of three or more letters that result in acceptable words. For example, in the following letter display, the word *jump* would be acceptable (as would *joy, job, you* and *ail* if all directions are allowed), but the word *on* is too short to be included:,

4. The students keep searching for words until the time runs out.
5. At the end of play, the groups add up their scores – one point per letter of an acceptable word. Record the results for the groups and declare the winning group.

Variations:
- Students can use the word grid with spaces (18.3). They can insert a letter that will help them to make a word (but once a letter has been inserted, it cannot be changed).
- Points are only given for words that are not duplicated by other groups.
- Students can use the blank template to make a game for others in the class.
- Each student in the group has a letter grid and works independently to find words, then students pool their results.

Word Search 1

A	Y	F	O	O	D	A	B	U	Y	F	O
O	E	A	S	T	A	E	O	A	U	E	V
F	A	S	T	E	F	U	O	S	A	W	A
Z	O	O	H	L	E	O	B	U	I	A	E
A	A	P	A	Y	H	I	E	T	A	G	I
G	X	A	I	B	I	E	Q	U	I	E	T
C	A	R	Y	E	S	R	D	I	B	E	S
H	V	E	A	U	I	B	W	D	C	X	Y
E	O	E	B	V	G	E	C	U	D	O	O
R	E	A	L	Y	T	P	J	U	M	P	G
E	N	E	R	G	Y	K	W	O	M	E	N
I	D	A	P	P	L	E	M	Q	U	I	T

Photocopiable

Word Search 2

18.2

S	T	A	Ɛ	O	A	U	I
T	Ɛ	F	U	O	S	A	T
A	Y	H	I	Ɛ	T	A	G
I	B	I	Ɛ	Q	U	C	I
Y	Ɛ	S	R	D	I	B	Ɛ
L	Y	T	P	J	U	M	P
R	G	Y	K	J	W	O	M
P	P	L	U	M	Ɛ	Q	U

Word Search 3

A			O	U	T	A	B		T	F	O
S	E	A		T	A		O	A	K	I	U
F	A		T	E	F	O			A	W	A
O	G	H		E	O	B	U		A	E	
S	A	P	A		H	I	E		A	G	I
G		A	I	B	I		Q	U			N
C	A		Y	E	S	R			B	E	S
H	V	E	A		I	B		D	C		Y
O	E	B		G	E	C		D		O	
R	E	A			T	P		U	M	P	G
E	N		R		Y	K	W	O		E	N
I		A	P	P	L	E	M			I	T

Photocopiable

Word Search – Template

Alphabet Soup

Game 19

Learning objective: To generate words.

Game objective:: To create the most new words.

Organization: Played in small groups of 3–4 students.

Preparation:
1. Copy one Game Board for each group of 3–4 students.
2. Provide each group with a watch or clock with a second hand or a timer.
3. Provide each student with one large or many smaller pieces of paper.

Description of the game:
1. The youngest student chooses any category on the board in which he/she thinks he/she knows a lot of words. The student who chooses the category is also the timekeeper.
2. All students in the group have one minute to think of and write down as many words as they can related to the category printed in the space. The words they write must contain at least one letter from the alphabet boxes touching the category on the board, e.g., for the category *body parts* (top left), the words generated must contain an A, M, L or P. Acceptable words would be <u>a</u>rm, <u>lip</u>, h<u>a</u>nd, f<u>a</u>ce, <u>palm</u>, e<u>a</u>r, <u>m</u>usc<u>l</u>e and shou<u>l</u>der, but *foot*, *nose* and *finger* wouldn't be acceptable, because they don't contain the target letters (*a, m, l, p*).
3. At the end of the minute, all words that are duplicated are crossed out – for example, if two students have written the word *lip* they must both cross is off their lists.
4. Then the students add up their points. They receive one point for each word containing a target letter. If a word has more than one target letter, the student receives one point for each target letter, e.g., <u>h</u>and is worth one point but <u>palm</u> is worth four points. Students keep track of their own points.
5. During a student's turn, he/she is responsible for keeping track of the time and leading the discussion of which words are acceptable. The teacher serves as moderator if there is any disagreement.
6. The categories are crossed out as they are used. The student to the left of the first student chooses a new category. That student is now responsible for keeping track of time and discussing acceptability of words.
7. Play continues with each student in turn choosing a new category.
   Note: Before the class starts playing, determine whether accurate spelling is required or not. If not, how inaccurate can the students be?

Variations:
- For more advanced classes, make the rules more interesting, e.g.: the person who chooses the category also determines a) the time limit, b) if the words may contain any of the target letters or only one or two letters, c) if the words must only contain the letter(s) or must *begin* with the target letters. The student must determine these rules before all players begin writing words, but the rules can change on each turn. The scoring rules remain the same.
- The students create words using the target letters but without categories. Give every student a sheet with the letters without the categories. Students make words containing the target letters from no particular category and write them in the spaces, e.g., in the box surrounded by A, M, L, and P, the student may write *lap, palm, map, pal*. Play as a class or model once and play in small groups.

Alphabet Soup – Game Board 1

A	M	C	T	W
body parts	animals	car words	colors	
L	P	H	E	K
music	travel	shopping	verbs	
I	T	Y	R	N
clothing	sports	food	family	
S	E	F	O	G
toys	adjectives	hobbies	class words	
D	B	P	U	C
time words	health	summer	house words	
S	E	L	N	J
cold things	computer words	movie words	fruit	
K	U	R	M	A
love	vegetables	work	winter	
O	D	V	S	I

Photocopiable

Alphabet Soup – Game Board 2

F	P	S	L	U
J	I	T	A	K
C	B	N	R	Y
G	E	S	O	E
H	P	W	U	T
S	O	N	D	M
K	C	E	I	F
A	D	V	M	A

Photocopiable

Alphabet Soup – Template

19.3

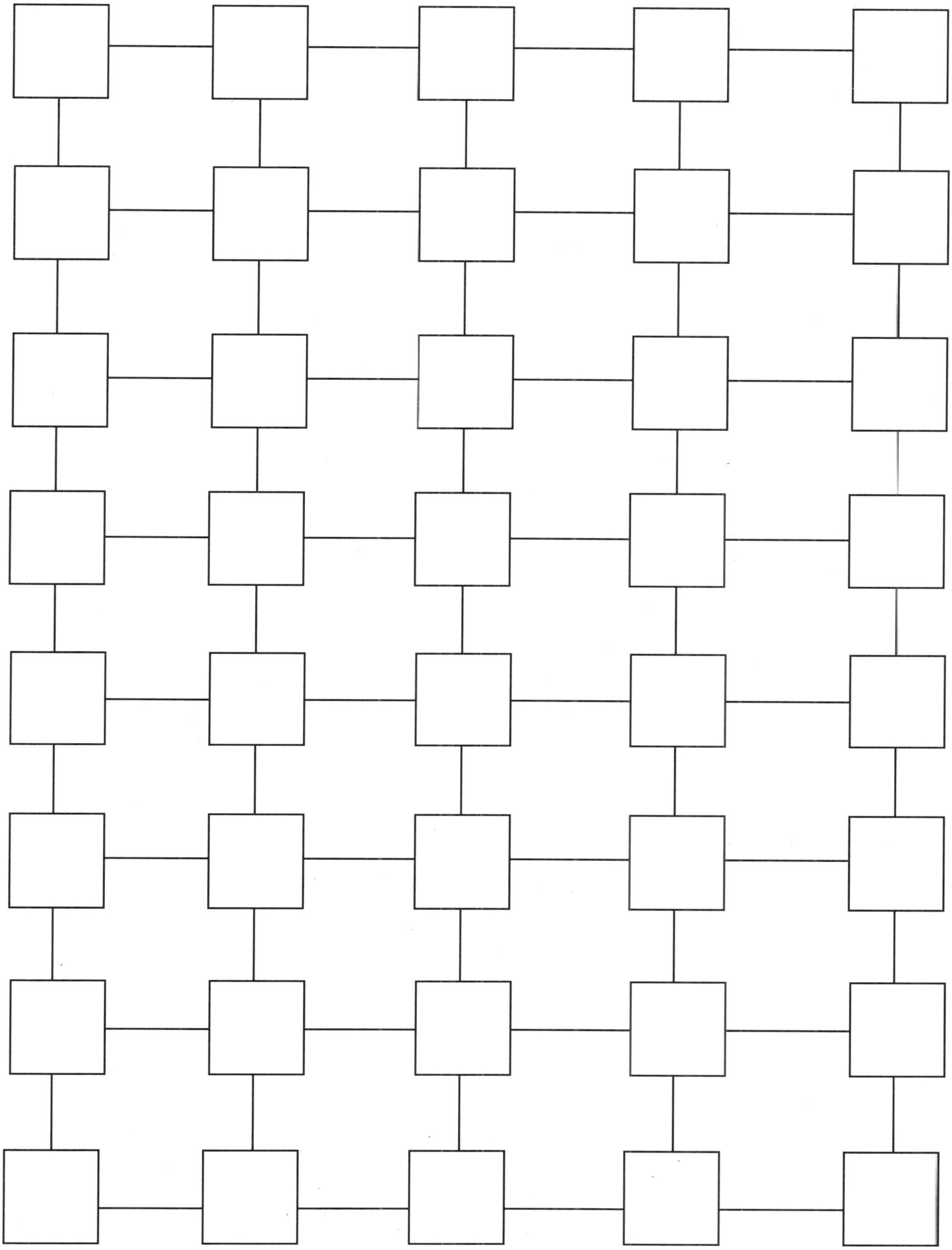

Photocopiable

Five in a Row

Game 20

Learning objective: To display knowledge of vocabulary and spelling by placing words diagonally in a grid according to the first letter of the word.

Game objective: To be the team with the highest number of claimed squares at the end of the game.

Organization: Played in groups.

Preparation:
1. Prepare small markers that are grey on one side and white on the other by using the pages that follow. Alternatively, you can find small flat markers with a different colour on each side, e.g., black on one side and white on the other.
2. Provide a Game Board and a set of small coloured markers for each team.

Description of the game:
1. Divide each group of students into teams. The students sit in a circle with the Game Board in the middle. Select one student to be the recorder for each group of two teams. The recorder keeps a list of words used; when a team repeats a word that has already been used, they miss a turn.
2. The objective is to claim five squares in a **diagonal** row (the starting letter of the word must appear on both the top and the side of the board) without being blocked by the other team.
3. In turn, each team claims a square by selecting it and giving a word that begins with that letter (e.g., if the letter "D" corresponds to the top and side of the grid, the team gives a word that begins with that letter). They then put their coloured marker on that square.

4. Squares do not have to be placed consecutively.
5. Teams can 'steal' the squares of the opposing team by bracketing **fewer than five squares** belonging to that team (i.e., placing one of their markers on each side of an opponent's markers to stop them from getting a row of five). The 'stealing' team then claims those squares and changes all the markers in between to their own colour.
6. Chains of five squares cannot be changed or stolen.
7. Words cannot be repeated. The recorder keeps a record of the words used and, if a team reuses a word, they forfeit their turn.
8. Play continues until all the possible squares have been claimed or until the time limit has been reached.

Variation:
- Students have to make a sentence with the target word before claiming the square.

Five in a Row – Backing for Markers 1

	B	C	D	F	G	H	J	K	L	M	N	P	R	S	T	W	
B																	W
C																	T
D																	S
F																	R
G																	P
H																	N
J																	M
K																	L
L																	K
M																	J
N																	H
P																	G
R																	F
S																	D
T																	C
W																	B
	W	T	S	R	P	N	M	L	K	J	H	G	F	D	C	B	

Photocopiable

Five in a Row – Backing for Markers 2

Five in a Row – Game Board

One of a Kind

Game

Learning objective: To generate target words.

Game objective: To be the player with the most new target words.

Organization: Played as a class.

Preparation: Copy a table for each student.

Description of the game:
1. Choose any letter of the alphabet, or have a student draw a letter out of bag or use the alphabet board in the front of this book. Everyone writes that letter in the first column of the table in row 1.
2. The students have one minute to think of a word beginning with the letter for each category in the columns of the table, e.g., if the letter is D a student can write *doughnut* for Food, *dog* for Animal, *doctor* for Job Title, *dress* for Clothing, *donkey* for Transportation, *depressed* for Feeling and *dancing* for Entertainment.
3. When the time is up, the students must put down their pens. The teacher asks what students wrote for the category Food. If any students wrote the same word, they must cross them out and they get no points for that category. Only the students who wrote a correct word that *no one else wrote* get a point. For example, one student reads their word: *doughnut*; the teacher asks if anyone else wrote *doughnut*; if another students says yes, neither student gets a point. If there is disagreement about whether a word fits a particular category, the teacher decides whether it counts or not. Points are written at the end of each row. The teacher must ask shy students what they wrote to ensure everyone's words are either unique or crossed out.
4. Play again with another letter of the alphabet, chosen at random.
   Note: It is important the letters are random or students 'cheat' by writing words ahead of time.

Variations:
- Change the categories by using the blank table provided.
- Change the time limit.
- Play in teams of 2–3 players.
- Make spelling count – or not.
- The teacher also plays, making it even more challenging for students.
- After one model round, the game is played in small groups, allowing the teacher time to do other activities with other students. Students can jump in and out of the game easily.

One of a Kind – Table

Letter	Food	Animal	Job Title	Clothing	Transportation	Feeling	Entertainment
1							
2							
3							
4							
5							
6							
7							
8							
9							
10							
11							
12							
13							
14							
15							
16							
17							
18							
19							
20							

Photocopiable

One of a Kind – Template

Letter	1	2	3	4	5	6	7	8	9	10	11	12	13	14	15	16	17	18	19	20

Photocopiable

Word List

A

abandon *(v)* to give up or leave
ability *(n)* something you can do
absence *(n)* not in a place; away
academic *(adj)* related to studying
acceptable *(adj)* good enough
access *(n)* right or chance to use something; *(v)* to find and use something
accurate *(adj)* correct or exact
achieve *(v)* to finish or do what you want
acknowledge *(v)* to give recognition or credit
acquisition *(n)* something that has been obtained
active *(adj)* busy; moving; full of energy
actually *(adv)* really
adequate *(adj)* sufficient; enough
adjustment *(n)* a change
admire *(v)* to have respect for and like something
advantage *(n)* something that helps or makes better
affect *(v)* do something to cause a change in something or someone
agreement *(n)* a decision that people make together
aim *(n)* a goal or purpose; *(v)* to try to hit or reach something exactly
alter *(v)* to change
alternative *(adj)* another choice; instead of
ambiguous *(adj)* not clear
ambition *(n)* a strong desire to do something
amendment *(n)* a change
analysis *(n)* thinking about or looking carefully at something
annoy *(v)* to bother or not be pleasant to others
apparent *(adj)* easy to see
appear *(v)* to become visible
approach *(v)* to come up to; to move closer to
appropriate *(adj)* suitable
arbitrarily *(adv)* randomly; without reason
area *(n)* 1. part of a city, country or the world; 2. size of a surface or place
arise *(v)* to come up; to be seen
arrangement *(n)* 1. a plan that has been agreed on; 2. the things you must plan in order for something to take place
aspect *(n)* part or piece
assessment *(n)* evaluation; judgement about ability
assistance *(n)* help
association *(n)* 1. a group of people; 2. a linking of ideas
assume *(v)* to believe something without confirmation
attitude *(n)* the way a person feels or thinks about something
authority *(n)* person or ruling party in control
available *(adj)* not busy; able to do something
avoid *(v)* try not to do something or see someone
aware *(adj)* knowing that something is true or exists
awkward *(adj)* not comfortable

B

baby *(n)* small child
baggage *(n)* luggage; bag; something to hold items
basically *(adv)* in the main and most important ways
basket *(n)* container made of dried grass
beat *(v)* 1. to hit hard; 2. to win against
behave *(v)* to act in a certain way
behaviour *(n)* the way a person or animal acts
beneficial *(adj)* helpful or useful
benefit *(n)* something that is helpful; *(v)* to help someone
boast *(v)* to talk about how good something is
border *(n)* 1. a line dividing two countries; 2. a band around the edge of something
bribe *(n)* money you pay to get what you want (usually illegal); *(v)* to pay money to get what you want (usually illegal)
building *(n)* structure with walls and a roof (e.g., house, factory)
bundle *(n)* group of things
business *(n)* company trying to make money

C

calculate *(v)* to find out about something using numbers
capably *(adv)* well
capacity *(n)* amount
career *(n)* working life; job
carry *(v)* to lift and take to another place
category *(n)* group of things or people that are similar in some way
cause *(n)* reason why something happens, *(v)* to make something happen
celebration *(n)* something special you do on an important day

central *(adj)* in the middle
century *(n)* 100 years
ceremony *(n)* formal set of actions used at an important social or religious event
certainly *(adv)* for sure; 100% positive
challenge *(n)* something new, exciting or difficult to do; *(v)* 1. to question if something is fair; 2. to dare someone to a fight or competition
chance *(n)* opportunity
chart *(n)* a picture or graph showing information; *(v)* to record information over time
chiefly *(adv)* mostly
circumstances *(n)* factors that affect a situation
clarify *(v)* to make clear or easy to understand
classical *(adj)* belonging to the past; based on traditions
clearly *(adv)* easily seen
client *(n)* customer
cliff *(n)* sharp drop from high ground to low ground
climate *(n)* usual weather in a particular area
coarse *(adj)* not smooth; rough
code *(n)* 1. secret symbols or letters used instead of ordinary words; 2. a set of rules that tell people how to live
collar *(n)* something that fits around a neck
combination *(n)* two or more things used or put together
commit *(v)* to do wholeheartedly; to promise time, money or energy
committee *(n)* group of people with a particular purpose
community *(n)* group of people living together or having a common belief
comparison *(n)* look at how two things are similar and different
compensation *(n)* something given as payment for an unpleasant action or service
complex *(n)* group of buildings belonging together
complex *(adj)* difficult; having many parts
comprehensive *(adj)* complete
concept *(n)* idea or abstract thought
conclusion *(n)* end
conclusive *(adj)* 1. showing something is true without a doubt; 2. ending something
condition *(n)* 1. state of being that someone or something is in; 2. something that must happen first before something else can
conference *(n)* large formal meeting
confess *(v)* to tell the truth; to admit to something

confirm *(v)* to ensure something is correct
conflict *(n)* disagreement
connection *(n)* relationship between people, things or events
consent *(v)* to agree
consent *(n)* agreement
consequences *(n)* things that happen as a result of actions
consider *(v)* to think about carefully
considerable *(adj)* large or important
consistent *(adj)* predictable and unchanging
constant *(adj)* not changing
constantly *(adv)* without stopping
constraints *(n)* restrictions; things that make something difficult to do
consult *(v)* ask for advice
context *(n)* situation (or circumstances) surrounding something
continuously *(adv)* without stopping
contrary *(adj)* opposite
control *(v)* to manage or direct something completely
conversation *(n)* talking and listening to another person
convert *(v)* to change
cooperative *(adj)* working well together; friendly
corporate *(adj)* related to business
corresponding *(adj)* matching or similar
create *(v)* to make something new
criteria *(n)* standards used to judge something
crucial *(adj)* very important; necessary
cruel *(adj)* mean; not nice
culture *(n)* ideas, art, customs and beliefs of a particular group of people or society
current *(adj)* at the present time
customer *(n)* person who pays for a service or product

D

dark *(adj)* without light
data *(n)* factual information
debate *(n)* discussion between people with different opinions; *(v)* to discuss a subject; to exchange opinions
decisively *(adv)* firmly; leaving no room for doubt
define *(v)* to give a clear meaning or direction
definitely *(adv)* unquestionably; for sure
demand *(n)* need or desire for something; *(v)* to state what you want with force
demonstrate *(v)* to show how to do something
derived *(adj)* coming from something else

descend (v) to come down from
desert (n) sandy land without much water
design (n) plan or drawing
design (v) to make a drawing or a plan
despite (prep) regardless of; without care for something
destination (n) place where someone or something is going
detect (v) to notice
develop (v) to make better or more complete
difficult (adj) not easy
discuss (v) to talk about
distinction (n) difference between things
division (n) 1. act of breaking something into pieces; 2. maths term for calculating how many times a smaller number fits into a larger number
domestic (adj) 1. related to the home; 2. not wild
dominant (adj) in control; strongest
dramatically (adv) with lots of emotion
during (adv) at the same time as something else

E
early (adv) sooner than expected; not late
earn (v) to get money or reward for working or doing something
easily (adv) done without difficulty
easy (adj) simple; not difficult
economic (adj) related to money or business
economy (n) 1. the way money, trade, and industry are organized in a particular country; 2. the careful use of money, time, products, etc.
education (n) process of teaching and learning
effect (n) result or reaction to something or someone
elastic (adj) able to stretch and then go back into place; (n) thing made of rubber that can stretch and return to shape
election (n) vote organized to make a decision
elements (n) parts of something
eliminate (v) to remove
emerge (v) to come out of
emphasis (n) stress or importance of something
empty (adj) not full; nothing inside
empty (v) to take everything out
enable (v) to allow someone to do something

energy (n) 1. ability to do a lot of work; 2. usable power (such as heat or electricity)
enforce (adj) to make better or more detailed enhanced; (v) make people follow a rule or law
enjoy (v) to like
ensure (v) to make sure
enter (v) to go in
entity (n) something that exists as a single, separate and complete unit
environment (n) 1. surroundings; 2. the land, water and air in which animals and people live
equivalent (n) something of equal value
error (n) mistake
especially (adv) particularly
established (adj) well-known or proven
evaluate (v) to judge if something is good or bad
event (n) something unusual or important that happens
eventually (adv) finally; over time
evidence (n) proof that something is true
evil (adj) not good; coming from the devil; (n) something that is not good
evolution (n) slow change over time
exact (adj) correct and accurate
example (n) something you use to show what you mean
exceed (v) to go beyond expectations
excluded (adj) not a part of
expensive (adj) costing a lot of money
expertly (adv) with special skill and knowledge; professionally
explain (v) to make clear and easy to understand
explode (v) to burst into small pieces
explorer (n) someone who goes to new places or does new things
external (adj) on the outside
extraordinary (adj) not ordinary; special

F
face (n) part of the body with mouth, eyes and nose
faint (adj) not strong; (v) to fall down because you are weak; to lose consciousness
favourite (adj) most special or important
feathers (n) light objects that cover birds
female (adj) being of woman or girl; (n) a woman or girl
final (adj) last (in a series)
finally (adv) at last
financial (adj) related to money

finite *(adj)* limited; having an ending point
firm *(adj)* not soft or weak; *(n)* company; business
flat *(adj)* without any high or low spots; level; *(n)* apartment or small space a person pays to live in
flavour *(n)* taste
flexible *(adj)* easily changeable
float *(v)* to stay on the surface of water
focus *(n)* subject that is given special attention; *(v)* 1. to bring into view; 2. to give special attention
follow *(v)* to come after
forget *(v)* to not remember
forgive *(v)* to not be angry with a person anymore
form *(n)* shape; *(v)* to make something into a particular shape
frequently *(adv)* often; regularly
friend *(n)* someone you like who is not family

G
general *(adj)* 1. common; shared by many people; 2. not specific; *(n)* an officer of high rank in the army
generate *(v)* to make or create something
glimpse *(n)* quick look or view; *(v)* to look at quickly
globally *(adv)* 1. around the world; 2. considering the whole situation
goal *(n)* something you want to do
group *(n)* several people or things
guarantee *(n)* promise, usually with some kind of payment agreed if it is broken; *(v)* to promise
guard *(n)* person who protects something or something; *(v)* to protect someone or something
guess *(n)* estimate; approximate; *(v)* to try to answer a question without knowing for sure answer to something you are not sure about
guilty *(adj)* ashamed because you know you are wrong

H
habit *(n)* something you do regularly
happen *(v)* to take place; occur
health *(n)* state of having a strong body without disease
help *(n)* something you do to make something easier for someone else; *(v)* to give support or try to make something better
hence *(adv)* therefore; for this reason
home *(n)* place where you live or come from
honest *(adj)* truthful
hopeful *(adj)* believing something can or will happen
humble *(adj)* modest; not thinking you are better than others
hypothesis *(n)* theory; unproven idea about something based on reason

I
ideal *(adj)* perfect
identically *(adv)* done in exactly the same way
identified *(adj)* found and categorized; named
idle *(adj)* very lazy; not hardworking
illegal *(adj)* not permitted by the law
imagine *(v)* to picture in your mind
immigration *(n)* official process of entering another country
implementation *(n)* process of making a plan happen
implication *(n)* 1. something you don't say directly but hope others will understand; 2. possible effect
imply *(v)* to make understood without saying directly
impose *(v)* to force something upon people
impossible *(adj)* not able to happen
individually *(adv)* related to only one person
inevitably *(adv)* certainly; definitely happening
initial *(adj)* first
injury *(n)* harm or damage
inquire *(v)* to ask
inquiry *(n)* question
insect *(n)* six-legged small animal or a bug
insert *(v)* to add into
instance *(n)* moment
instant *(adj)* 1. at the same time; quickly; 2. made from powder
intelligent *(adj)* very smart, clever
interaction *(n)* activity of working or talking together
internal *(adj)* found inside
intervention *(n)* act of doing something that stops someone else from doing something
invent *(v)* to make something new
invite *(v)* to ask someone to do something with you
involvement *(n)* act of doing something or taking part in something
issue *(n)* something to be discussed (usually a problem); *(v)* to give or produce officially

J

jealous *(adj)* 1. wanting something someone else has; 2. not trusting
job *(n)* something you work at for money
journey *(n)* trip; *(v)* to take a trip

K

key *(adj)* important or main; *(n)* 1. object used to open a lock; 2. main idea or point; 3. list of explanations on a map; 4. button on a computer
knock *(v)* to hit something
knowledge *(n)* information
known *(adj)* something everyone knows

L

language *(n)* way of communicating ideas with sounds or writing
layer *(n)* one thickness, usually placed on top of another surface
leaf *(n)* green flat piece found on plants
learn *(v)* to study and remember
legal *(adj)* permitted by the law
legislation *(n)* law or set of laws
liberal *(adj)* 1. open minded; 2. free
light *(adj)* opposite of dark; *(n)* a bright spot; *(v)* to make something bright or on fire
liquid *(adj)* flowing; *(n)* something that can flow; not solid or gas
listen *(v)* to hear or pay attention to what someone says
location *(n)* place where something is found
lodging *(n)* place to stay
long *(adj)* measuring a great length; opposite of *short*
look *(v)* to see
loss *(n)* something you don't have anymore
loyal *(adj)* trustworthy; never changing your feeling for someone or something

M

mainly *(adv)* mostly; most importantly
maintain *(v)* to keep in good condition
major *(adj)* most important or largest
majority *(n)* most of the people or things in a particular group
male *(adj)* being of man or boy; *(n)* a man or boy
manage *(v)* to control and organize
map *(n)* picture of where things are
maximum *(adj)* largest allowed or possible; *(n)* most or largest amount allowed
maybe *(adv)* possibly; perhaps
medicine *(n)* drugs taken to improve your health
memory *(n)* 1. ability to remember things; 2. something you remember
mend *(v)* to fix
mental *(adj)* about the mind
mercy *(n)* capacity to forgive
minimally *(adv)* of the smallest amount possible
miserable *(adj)* very unhappy
modern *(adj)* the most recent or newest
modified *(adj)* changed
motivate *(v)* to get others to work or want something
move *(v)* to change position
multiply *(v)* to increase in number
music *(n)* sounds that are put together in a pattern
mystery *(n)* something that is unknown

N

naturally *(adv)* happening as a result of nature
nature *(n)* everything in the world not made or controlled by people
necessarily *(adv)* importantly
need *(v)* to feel that you must have something
negative *(adj)* seeing things badly; opposite of *positive*
neutral *(adj)* not taking sides
new *(adj)* not old
night *(n)* not day; when the sun is down
normal *(adj)* average; like others
notice *(v)* to see, feel or hear something or someone
number *(n)* e.g., 1, 2, 3

O

objective *(n)* goal or plan
objective *(adj)* not influenced by personal beliefs or feelings
obvious *(adj)* easy to see or understand
obviously *(adv)* easily seen
occupation *(n)* 1. job; 2. something you spend your time doing
occur *(v)* to take place; happen
offer *(n)* something someone says they'll do for you; *(v)* to ask someone if they want you to do something
once *(adv)* one time
open *(v)* to make accessible
opinion *(n)* ideas or beliefs

opportunity *(n)* chance to do something you want to do
option *(n)* choice
organized *(adj)* well-planned or arranged
origin *(n)* 1. where something came from; 2. the reason why something started
original *(adj)* first

P

pale *(adj)* very light in colour
parallel *(adj)* running next to each other but always the same distance apart
parameters *(n)* limits that control how something can be done
particular *(adj)* exactly or especially this one
pause *(n)* moment to wait; short break; *(v)* to wait for a moment
perceived *(adj)* seen as
per cent *(n)* number in each 100
perform *(v)* 1. to do something to entertain; 2. to do a task
period *(n)* a length of time
permanent *(adj)* lasting forever or a long time
personal *(adj)* 1. belonging to or related to you 2. private
phase *(n)* a step or phase in a process
physical *(adj)* related to the body
plan *(n)* something you expect to do; *(v)* 1. to expect to do something; 2. to get ready
policy *(n)* official way of doing something
poor *(adj)* 1. without much money; not rich; 2. not good
population *(n)* number of people living in a particular place
positive *(adj)* happy; considering the good things; not negative
possible *(adj)* can happen; maybe
potential *(adj)* possible
powder *(n)* small dry pieces or grains
power *(n)* energy or strength
precious *(adj)* very important and valuable to someone
predict *(v)* to guess what will happen
predominantly *(adv)* mostly; strongly
preference *(n)* something you like more than other things
prejudice *(n)* unfair feeling against someone
pressure *(n)* 1. attempt to make someone do something; 2. force or weight put on something
prevent *(v)* to stop from happening
previous *(adj)* coming before
previously *(adv)* beforehand
primarily *(adv)* firstly or most importantly
prior *(adj)* coming before
probable *(adj)* likely to happen
process *(n)* something done step by step; *(v)* to do something step by step;
produce *(v)* to make something, usually to sell
professionally *(adv)* 1. very well (because you have training); 2. for payment or as part of a job
prohibit *(v)* to not allow
promise *(n)* statement that you will definitely do something; *(v)* to say for sure you will do something
proud *(adj)* feeling that something is very good
psychology *(n)* study of the mind
public *(adj)* evident to everyone; not private; *(n)* people in general
publish *(v)* 1. to make information available to everyone; 2. to have a book or article available to buy
published *(adj)* printed in a book, magazine or newspaper
purchase *(v)* to buy
pursue *(v)* to chase or look for

Q

qualify *(v)* 1. to succeed at a task that makes you able to do something else; 2. to add information
quarrel *(v)* to disagree; *(n)* disagreement
quotation *(n)* something someone else says, repeated word for word

R

radically *(adv)* extremely
raise *(v)* to make higher or bigger
randomly *(adv)* in no particular order
rapidly *(adv)* quickly
ration *(n)* limited amount of something
razor *(n)* sharp blade, usually used to cut hair
reaction *(n)* something that happens because of something else
realization *(n)* act of knowing something you didn't know before
recent *(adj)* a short time ago
recognize *(v)* to know something because you knew it before
recommend *(v)* to tell others that something or someone is good
recover *(v)* to get better
regime *(n)* ruling party or government
registered *(adj)* listed with an official organization
regularly *(adv)* often; frequently

regulations *(n)* official rules
reinforce *(v)* 1. to make stronger; 2. to state again
relationship *(n)* connection between people or things
relevant *(adj)* related to the topic being discussed
reliably *(adv)* trustworthily; without failing
reliance *(n)* state of being dependent on something
relieve *(v)* 1. to help someone; 2. to replace someone
remain *(v)* to stay in one place
remember *(v)* to keep in one's mind; not forget
remind *(v)* to tell someone again so they don't forget
repeat *(v)* to say or do again
required *(adj)* needed
research *(n)* study of something to find information; *(v)* to study something to find new information
resident *(n)* someone who lives in a place
resist *(v)* to try to stop something happening
respectful *(adj)* polite to others
respond *(v)* to answer
response *(n)* answer
responsible *(adj)* 1. trustworthy; 2. in charge of something
restore *(v)* to put in order; to put together again
restricted *(adj)* not open to everyone; open to a specific group
retained *(adj)* kept back
retire *(v)* to not work anymore
revenue *(n)* money earned by a business
review *(v)* to look at again
revision *(n)* 1. change to something; 2. act of studying
rich *(adj)* having a lot of money
role *(n)* 1. the position or function of something; 2. the part played
room *(n)* 1. part of a building that has its own walls; 2. enough space to do something

S

scheme *(n)* a plan; *(v)* to plan
scold *(v)* to tell someone what they did wrong
section *(n)* part of something
sector *(n)* part of a specific system or society
secure *(adj)* safe; *(v)* to make safe
select *(v)* to choose
selective *(adj)* choosy; only taking the best parts
sequence *(n)* series or order of things
series *(n)* group of things that come one after another
several *(adj)* more than a few; not many
shift *(v)* to move
significant *(adj)* important or large
similar *(adj)* alike
similarity *(n)* almost the same
simple *(adj)* easy
simulation *(n)* practice of what can or will happen
small *(adj)* little; opposite of big
social *(adj)* mixing with other people
solution *(n)* answer to a problem
sore *(adj)* hurt and tired
sought *(adj)* looked for
source *(n)* origin or starting point
speak *(v)* to talk
splendid *(adj)* excellent; very good
stability *(n)* condition of being steady or not changing
statistics *(n)* numbers representing facts or measurements
status *(n)* ranking; position in society
steady *(adj)* happening or moving in a slow and gradual way
stop *(v)* to not do anymore
straight *(adj)* directly; not bent or curved
strategies *(n)* ways of trying to do something
subsequent *(adj)* following
substitution *(n)* something used instead of something else
successful *(adj)* having done what you wanted; having a good job and money
sudden *(adj)* quick; unexpected
suffer *(v)* to feel unhappy or in pain
sufficient *(adj)* enough
summary *(n)* short version
supportive *(adj)* helpful
surface *(n)* outside part of something
survive *(v)* to live through
sympathy *(n)* feeling of support for someone who is hurt or unhappy

T

tame *(adj)* not wild; domesticated; *(v)* to make an animal safe around people
technical *(adj)* involving expert knowledge
techniques *(n)* ways of doing something
tempt *(v)* to try to get someone to do something
tender *(adj)* soft; not hard
tensely *(adv)* done with stress, nerves or not moving freely

text *(n)* written material
theory *(n)* reasonable idea that hasn't been proven
thereby *(adv)* by that; connected with
tight *(adj)* pulled or stretched so that something is straight; not loose
topic *(n)* main idea; subject
totally *(adv)* completely; wholly
trade *(n)* business of buying and selling; *(v)* to buy and sell
tradition *(n)* belief, custom or way of doing something that started in the past
traditional *(adj)* following ideas or customs from the past
train *(v)* 1. to teach someone; 2. to learn something
trend *(n)* the way things are generally going
true *(adj)* based on facts; opposite of *false*
trustworthy *(adj)* reliable; likely to do the honest thing

U

ugly *(adj)* not beautiful; not nice to look at
ultimately *(adv)* finally
unbelievably *(adv)* incredibly
underlying *(adj)* behind something
uniformly *(adv)* without changing; evenly
unique *(adj)* special and different from anything else
urge *(v)* to try to get someone to do something
usually *(adv)* most of the time
utility *(n)* something that is made to be useful

V

valid *(adj)* founded on truth or fact
valuable *(adj)* having a lot of worth; important to someone
variable *(n)* factor that affects something else
variety *(n)* different things
view *(n)* 1. opinion; 2. what someone can see
virtually *(adv)* almost completely
visibly *(adv)* in a way that others can see
volume *(n)* 1. amount of something; 2. level of noise

W

warn *(v)* to tell someone about danger or a problem
water *(n)* liquid in rain, oceans, rivers and seas
witness *(n)* someone who saw something happen; *(v)* to see something happen (e.g., a crime)
work *(v)* 1. to do a job for money; 2. to do something that takes effort
work *(n)* job you are paid to do
world *(n)* the Earth
worry *(v)* to be concerned; to think about someone or something often
wrap *(v)* to cover with a cloth or paper
write *(v)* to use a pen or pencil to form letters or words